HERE COMES THE BRIDE

Other Books By Ken McDonald

Pursuit
One Man's Quest to Find God's Perfect Will for His Life

Defiled
The Spiritual Dangers of Alternative Medicine

Jesus Talk To Me
Have you ever desired to get God's attention?
(Sermon in a Book Series, Vol. 1)

Dealing With Bad In-Laws
A Bible study on Jacob and Laban

HERE COMES THE BRIDE

A Critique of the Baptist Bride Heresy

KEN MCDONALD, B.D., Th.M.

Every Word Publishing
Pensacola, Florida

©2015 Every Word Publishing

All Rights Reserved. No part of this publication may be reproduced, stored in a retrieval system, or transmitted in any form by any means, electronic, mechanical, photocopy, recording, or otherwise, without the prior written permission of the pubisher, except for brief quotations in critical reviews or articles.

All Scripture quotations are from the King James Version and any mistakes in the quotation are not intended.

Published in the United States of America by Every Word Publishing
Every Word Publishing
PO Box 2428, PMB #24476
Pensacola, FL 32513

info@everywordpublishing.com

First Edition (ISBN 978-0-9798844-1-2):
First Printing 2001- 500 copies
Second Printing 2008 - 2000 copies
Second Edition 2015 (ISBN 978-0-9798844-5-0)

Cover design: Rebekah McDonald Maxim
Image Copyright Lai Len Yiap, 2007
Used under license from www.FeaturePics.com

DEDICATION

This book is dedicated to those Christians who have been willing to exercise their individual soul liberty in Jesus Christ, based on the rightly divided word, so that they have been led by the Holy Spirit, according to the word of God, and not according to what some one has told them to do, or believe.

Though often maligned, and accused of being rebellious, backslidden, or lost, yet they have dared to stand on the word of God, alone! As I heard one Filipino Christian put it, who had come out of a Baptist Brider Church and was now a member of a Bible Believing Baptist Church, "It's good to be free!" Amen and Amen!!!

Contents

Introduction 9

Chapter 1
The Heresy In Their Own Words 19

Chapter 2
The Standing and State of the Believer 37

Chapter 3
Your State 63

Chapter 4
The Difference Between the Physical
and the Spiritual 85

Chapter 5
Seven Baptisms 113

Chapter 6
Seven Baptisms Part II 135

Chapter 7
The Similarities Between the Nicolaitans
and the Briders 151

Chapter 8
So, Why Be Baptist? 159

INTRODUCTION

THE BAPTIST BRIDE HERESY

It was around 1983 when I first encountered a pastor who was a Baptist Brider. I had just arrived in Modesto, a town of about 150,000 people, and with great zeal I was going to set the world on fire. Oh, I was excited!

There was an independent Baptist church across town, and I wanted to meet the pastor. I wanted to let him know that I would be starting a church on the other side of town, and that I in no way would be trying to take any of his people or cause him any trouble. I gave him a call and went over on a certain day to see him.

The conversation went well, with the usual small talk, until he asked me by what authority was I starting a church. I thought to myself, "By what authority? There are people dying and going to Hell around here, and he is asking by what authority was I starting a church?"

I told him that my authority was the word of God. His reply completely astounded me. With an emphatic voice he thundered, "No, sir! No, sir! That's not your authority. The local church is your authority. You have no authority to start a church!"

I thought, "You mean the local church has more authority than the word of God?"

According to him, I was not going about the work of the Lord scripturally. I needed to be sent out by a local church. Well, I had been sent out by my home church, but to those of us who are not Briders the word of God gives us the authority, and takes precedence over the local church.

He said, "In the book of Acts, chapter 13:1-4, it was the local church that sent the men out."

Have you read what the Bible says in the Book of Acts? Notice in verse 4 the Bible says, "...they, being sent forth by the Holy Ghost...". It doesn't say, "the local church." It says, "by the Holy ghost." The word of God says what it means and means what it says. tFor many years, I have thought about that conversation and wondered why he would say such a thing. As I have come in contact with more and more Briders, I now know that this is one of the marks of Briderism - Church Authority!

> "The Lord instituted and commissioned His church to carry out His work. Only New

Introduction

Testament churches are authorized to plant New Testament churches."

<small>Les Potter, *The Mystical Invisible Universal "Church"*, (Calvary Publishing, Lansing MI) 64</small>

Ah yes! Authority! Briders believe that you don't have the authority to plant a church, only "we" do. You don't have the authority to baptize either, and you don't have the authority to assemble, preach etcetera. Only we do. (But we will let you tithe!)

Who is that? The Baptists! Which ones? The true Baptists! You are not qualified because you are not a proper Baptist and therefore you do not have the authority to do the great commission.

Did you ever think about this? What was the grounds for crucifying Jesus Christ? John 19:7 *"The Jews answered him, We have a law, and by our law he ought to die, because he made himself the Son of God."* Their grounds for crucifying Him was that **He was not qualified.** Who said that? The religious leaders said that.

The truth is Jesus Christ was THE ONLY One ever qualified to do anything for God. Nobody is ever completely qualified. The only thing all men have ever been qualified for is to die and sink in the lake of fire. Anything aside from that is by the goodness and grace of God.

Again I came across another man who, when I met him, had been in the ministry quite a number of years. (Watch out for older preachers who have been around for a while, and tell you something different than what you received from the words that came from the mouth of God, 1 Kings 13.) He had started a church and, because of a tragedy in his family, was in the process of looking for another preacher to come and take the work over. I filled the pulpit for him a number of times and eventually pastored the work for a short time.

I noticed that when he preached he talked a lot about John the Baptist. As I talked to him one day, he stated that the church goes back to John the Baptist, and you had to be a member of the local Baptist church to be in the Bride of Christ.

It then hit me that he was a Brider. "Oh!" he said, "if you'll ever understand that truth you will be shouting, Glory!" He said it was one of the happiest days of his life when he realized that the Baptist Church was the Bride of Christ and that he was in the bride. I mentioned to him there were some contrasts between the Body of Christ and the local church, but it was to no avail.

Then things started to make sense. I had gone to a fellowship a few weeks earlier and met a man who was the pastor of another church. His church was the sponsor, or mother church, of the little church I now pastored.

(Isn't it strange how when a man or woman believes in a heresy, they have a hard time telling people what they really believe? The Mormons don't go around telling people they believe Jesus Christ and the Devil are brothers, or that they believe they will be gods one day. They go around with a Bible making you think

Introduction

they are good Christians, and believe the same things Christians believe. They are lying wolves coming to you in sheep's clothing. The Briders will not say they are Briders. They have the hardest time telling you what they really believe. You have to pry it out of them in the back room.)

Now back to the story. He said that the church had to have a sponsor so that the line of authority would be there. I suppose, then, they could trace it all the way back to John the Baptist, the one true church. Yes, the Baptist church is the one true church? So they say.

This was my introduction into the heresy of Baptist Briderism. Since then, I have come across this teaching in many different Baptist churches. Some of the pastors don't even know that they are espousing the views of the Baptist Briders. Often it comes through intimidation.

A pastor will start making statements that assert more and more strongly how right the Baptists are. His fellow pastors will pressure him into thinking that to believe all Christians are in the Bride of Christ is to be liberal, or a compromiser. If you believe all the saved are in the Bride then you are making Jesus Christ an adulterer. Through intimidation and lack of Bible study, the pastor will go along with the crowd of fellow pastors and begin to espouse heresy.

I've found that the average preacher is scared to death to stand alone. I'm talking about the "INDEPENDENT" preachers. Many of them seem to huddle around in groups like a covey of quail. Instead of basing their actions and beliefs on what the word of God says, they will look to each other. Oftentimes going along with their school or the preacher that has the largest church. (2 Cor. 10:12,*"...but they measuring themselves by themselves, and comparing themselves among themselves, are not wise."*)

In my life and in my ministry, I have found this to be true: If you are going to go on the light that God gives you from the word of God, and only the truths that line up with the word of God, you had better be prepared to be in a minority. It will also be a life that will make people mad. When you go by the book, you will often go against the majority. The majority is always wrong (Matt. 7:13-14,*"...broad is the way, that leadeth to destruction, and many there be which go in thereat"*). Although there is no substitute for a clear conscience and fellowship with God.

As we get into this study we will accept what the word of God says. That is, the Authorized Version 1611 is the final authority in all matters of faith and practice. The King James Bible is God's preserved word and has stood the test of time. When a man or a church goes against the word of God, rightly divided, then that man or church is wrong.

In order to know what is right or wrong, you must have the word of God as the standard that judges what is right and what is wrong. God has preserved his word for all to read in the King James BIBLE, not "version." There are many "versions" which are translated from corrupt manuscripts producing corrupt translations. These are producing a corrupt

Introduction

Laodicean Christianity, which will end up right back in Rome with the mother of harlots.

Yes, it is the corrupt Roman Catholic text that is the basis for virtually all of the modern versions of the Bible. When a person goes to a Greek New Testament manuscript, 99% of the time it turns out to be a corrupt text. Even if they go to the Masoretic text, or one of the Received text manuscripts underlying the A.V., it still is not the inerrant word of God.

Acts 12:4, for example, in the King James Bible reads "Easter." This was one of John R. Rice's big "proofs" of mistakes in the King James Bible. He did not believe it was the inerrant word of God, and he would correct it often, just as the majority of apostate fundamentalists do today. His big argument was the Greek word in Acts 12:4 was "Pascal" and when properly translated it should read, "Passover."

What he failed to notice was the passage in verse three which states, *"Then were the days of unleavened bread."* If you study your Bible you will find that the Passover occurred at the start of the feast of unleavened bread and therefore the Passover had already passed (Lev. 23:4-5).

If you have a Bible that reads "Passover" instead of "Easter" then you have a mistake in your Bible. Easter is the proper word. It was Herod who was "intending" and would not "intend" after a Jewish feast, but would "intend" after a pagan feast, since he was a pagan. Your King James Bible is more accurate than "the Greek."

This is completely in line with Psalms 12:6-7,

15

"*Purified seven times.*" Scholars look at the word of God as being given perfectly, and that over the ages corruptions have entered and there is no longer an inerrant copy of the word of God left on the face of the earth. But the word of God says that the word has been, "*Purified seven times.*"

Not only has it been inspired but it has been IMPROVED UPON IN THE PROCESS OF PRESERVATION. The final text was given in 1611 in the Authrized Version. Though scholars try to throw up in the Bible believer's face that the King James Version has been updated many times since it came out, let it be stated that the text has not been changed. The text of 1611 has remained the same over the years. The new perversions of the Bible are not updates of the King James, but they are new versions that have completely changed the text.

In this study on the heresy of Baptist Briderism, we will not go to "the Greek" to try to prove a doctrine, as some of the Briders do when they get to 1 Cor. 12:13. It doesn't read as THEY THINK IT SHOULD. They go to the Greek to change the word of God; to make it fit in line with their heresy. They set themselves up as the final authority and usurp power over the word of God.

To a Brider, the local church, the pastor, church history, or "the Greek" is the final authority. That's because the Bible doesn't teach what they believe, so they have to go to another authority. The problem is that those are false authorities, and the word of God is the one true authority that all others must eventually answer to (Rev. 19:13, 20:11-15).

Lastly, before we get into the study of Briderism I will say that I am a Baptist, an independent Bible believing Baptist. I believe that the Baptists are the most scriptural out of all of the denominations. The issue, as with all things is, "What saith the scripture?" Though, as we will cover later, they have not been the ones who have been used by God to bring about worldwide revivals or nationwide revivals.

Proper scriptural position means little without proper application of those truths to the lives of the people who believe them. To sit and proclaim we're right, but fail to put what you believe into practice, is to be a deceived Pharisee and end up being put on a shelf by God.

Proper doctrine has to do, not only with head knowledge, but also with the application of that knowledge in the daily walk of the believer (Rom. 6:17, 2 Tim. 3:10, Titus 2:1). God has demonstrated over the years that He would rather use an ex-Roman Catholic priest than a Pharisee who has his doctrine right, but lacks charity, that is, a real love for, and subjection to, God and his word.

Here Comes The Bride

CHAPTER 1

THE HERESY:

IN THEIR OWN WORDS

According to their belief: The local independent Baptist church, or baptistic church, is the bride of Christ. To them, the Bride is referred to in Rev. 19:7-9:

> "7 Let us be glad and rejoice, and give honour to him: for the marriage of the Lamb is come, and his wife hath made herself ready. 8 And to her was granted that she should be arrayed in fine linen, clean and white: for the fine linen is the righteousness of saints. 9 And he saith unto me, Write, Blessed are they which are called unto the marriage supper of the Lamb. And he saith unto me, These are the true sayings of God."

The following is a list of quotes from men who are

pastors or teachers and who believe the local Baptist church is the bride of Christ. As such, then, I classify them as "Briders".

In his book titled, *The Myth of The Universal Invisible Church Theory Exploded!*, Roy Mason states:

> "It will then be revealed that the Bride will be composed of all the saved ones of those local, visible assemblies who have witnessed for Christ and carried on His work, gathered together in one happy group.
>
> He started this assembly, and in Matthew 16:18, promised to be with it and perpetuate it. We hear about them, read about them, and find evidence of the existence all through the centuries. That word Anabaptist was mockingly applied to them during much of the time. *THE "ANA" WAS FINALLY DROPPED* [emphasis added], but the people - the assemblies are the same.
>
> "There will be no mockery, no reproach, when at that festive gathering designated "the marriage Supper of the Lamb," our wonderful Lord presents His Bride and says, "I wish to present my beloved wife!"
>
> Roy Mason, *The Myth of The Universal Invisible Church Theory E-X-P-L-O-D-E-D!* (Little Rock, Arkansas: Challenge Press, 1978)79

Dr. Thomas Cassidy, Pastor of the First Baptist Church in Spring Valley, California, states in his article titled, "The Bride, the Baptists and the Bride of Christ:"

"...Eph. 4:4-5, There is one body, and one Spirit, even as ye are called in one hope of your calling; One Lord, one faith, one baptism...." It is obvious here that the Bible clearly teaches there is only one body. This passage does not indicate a NUMERICAL (emphasis added) singleness, but a TYPICAL (emphasis added) singleness. By this I mean there is only one TYPE of true New Testament church (called the body in Col. 1:18). We must now ask ourselves a question. Which TYPE of church is the true New Testament church? Is it the 'universal, invisible' church of liberal ecumenical protestantism, or the local, visible church of the Independent Baptists?

"When we see the term 'Body of Christ', we often forget this term is a METAPHOR used to illustrate truth concerning the true New Testament church. The term "Body" when referring to the church is never used in a mystical fashion, but is used simply as an identifier.

"The term 'Body of Christ' is simply a way to illustrate the relationship between Jesus Christ and His local, New Testament churches. *All of the redeemed will not be part of the Bride, but only those members of the family of God who have proved their love for the Lord through true obedience to His Word, by being faithful to His true New Testament church, and all that church* membership entails. [Emphasis added]

"The Bible says there will be a General Assembly in heaven; that is, a group of people who are not represented by, or under the authority of, any of the organized specific assemblies. The Bible clearly identifies the specific Assembly as the local New Testament church...[uses Hebrews 12:22-24]. This heavenly 'General Assembly' are clearly those folks from the gospel era who were saved, but were never baptized into the membership of, and faithful to, any of the Lord's specific assemblies, the New Testament churches.

"...the Church of the First Born is that group of saved, baptized people who were members of, and faithful to, the Lord's (the First Born, Col, 1:18) true New Testament churches.

"We see, therefore, that the Bride of Christ is not all of the redeemed, nor even all of the saved from the Gospel Era (Church Age), but only those faithful members of true New Testament churches.

"WAIT A MINUTE!!! It sounds to me like the writer of this article is a 'Baptist Brider.' That depends on what you think a 'Baptist Brider' is.

"If the average Christian is asked for a definition of the 'Baptist Bride' position, he would be hard pressed to give an intelligible answer. Some would say the 'Baptist Bride' position means 'Only Baptists are going to Heaven.'

"Others would say, 'Only Baptists will be raptured.' Others would say only, 'I don't know.' If the Baptist Bride position means only Baptists are going to heaven, then I'm not a Baptist Brider.

"If the Baptist Bride position means only Baptists will be raptured (partial rapture theory), then I'm not a Baptist Brider (nowhere does the Bible ever teach the 'rapture of the

Church', but it does teach the rapture of the saints, all of them: Old Testament saints, New Testament saints, church members, and non-church members, all will be caught up to meet the Lord in the air). But if you believe the Baptist Bride position means the Bride of Christ will be made up of those who have been faithful to the true (Baptistic, comment added) New Testament church of Jesus Christ, then, yep, I'm a Baptist Brider! I have to be. You see, I believe the Bible - all of it! The Bible says the Bride is the Church. It also says the Church is local and visible. If you have a local, visible church, then you must also have a local visible Bride, for the Bible teaches they are one and the same thing. If you have a universal Bride, you must also have a universal church, for they are still one and the same thing!

"Why is all of this so important? If we win souls, but do not make every effort possible to baptize them into local New Testament Baptist churches, and teach them to be faithful to the local New Testament church, we cheat those precious souls out of their full reward (emphasis added) (2 John 1:8). A proper understanding of the true New Testament church is absolutely necessary in order for our church members to realize *it is their faithfulness to their local church that will enable them to be called out of the family of God and placed into the Bride of Christ following the judgment seat of Christ, at the Marriage feast of the Lamb, and receive their full reward.* (Emphasis added) Every pastor must be made to understand that his job is to: Pray, Prepare, Preach, Protect, Preserve, and Perfect the Flock. The pastor's final task will be to present *the*

> church, the Bride of Christ, faultless, a chaste virgin, to the Bridegroom, the Lord Jesus Christ, at the Marriage Feast of the Lamb. (Emphasis added) "THINK ABOUT IT."
> Dr. Thomas Cassidy, *The Bride, the Baptists, and the Bride of Christ* (California: Spring Valley,1995)

Now, that is straight from the horse's mouth so to speak. One of the things a Baptist Brider believes is that his local independent Baptist church is the bride of Jesus Christ. That is where we get the term "Brider."

> Pg 77 "Our position is simply the historic Baptist position." Pg 35 "...Our conception of how Christ gave Himself for a local New Testament church is often nullified as a result of the popular universal church doctrine.
> "<u>Let the reader not miss the importance of this.</u> The local church is meant to perceive its relationship with its espoused head."
> Les Potter, *The Mystical Invisible Universal "Church"*, (Calvary Publishing, Lansing MI)77, 35

The local New Testament church that Bro. Potter is refering to is a Baptist church, based upon the historic Baptist position, or tradition. To be espoused means you are going to be married.

From the Central Baptist Church in Cincinnati, Ohio, Pastor James R. Love in an article titled, *The Bride*, printed in the publication, "The Flaming Torch", writes:

> 'This is a great mystery, but I speak concerning Christ and the church' (Ephesians 5:32). "We are going to look at a great mystery;

the relationship of Christ and His Bride in light of the first century wedding event. It is clear from the context of our text that the Bride is Christ's church.

"There are many different churches out there, but God is not a polygamist, as the Universal Church theory promotes. There is only one bride and I *believe the true Baptist church is it.* [Emphasis added]

"Baptists today may be classified as wall flowers or party poopers, but some day we, the Bride of Christ, are going to 'party hearty' at our supper.

"The New Testament church that Jesus established *is the Bride of Christ. Any church that does not follow that structure is not pure and cannot have the relationship with the Bridegroom. This includes any saved person that is not part of the true church.* [Emphasis added]

"The Bride today is to prepare herself for the voice of the Bridegroom when he calls out to her! The procession is nearing, we can hear the music of the last days. The church must bathe herself, cleanse herself, be dressed for our Bridegroom. It is time for churches to clean up!"

<small>Pastor James R. Love, *"The Bride,"* The Flaming Torch, October, November, December, 1995, (Rio Rancho, New Mexico)1,10-11</small>

Dr. Ron Tottingham, pastor of the Empire Baptist Temple in Sioux Falls, South Dakota, in his article, *"Baptist Brideism Is What?",* states:

"This Preacher believes that the Baptist faith and practice is the ONLY faith and practice true to the Scriptures. And that the being (That he might present it to himself a glorious church, not having spot, or wrinkle, or any such thing; but that it should be holy and without blemish, Ephesians 5:27) is more than just being born again.

"That TRUE doctrinal purity is what God points to as the final qualifier for His bride. Where is that in any other faith or practice? The Scriptures declare that the churches are synonymously the body of Christ.

"If the church and the body of Christ are synonymous, and are local, and are completed (not in prospect) fulfilling the designed purpose within this very age, to be rewarded in eternity; could being

THE Bride, Christ's bride, be that reward - perhaps for her zeal for being a soundly faithful church?"

Dr. Ron Tottingham, *"Baptist Brideism Is What?"*, (The Flaming Torch, October, November, December, 1995)7,13

In his booklet, *The Church,* Eld. Wayne Cox makes some very interesting comments:

Page 3
"It goes without saying that I believe the Bible is a Baptist Book - that it was written by Baptists, for Baptists, and to Baptists; and it will make Baptists of any who will read it with an unbiased and unprejudiced heart."

Page 4
"I take the position that Christ established His church during his personal ministry and *THAT*

IT WAS A BAPTIST CHURCH... [Emphasis added],"

Page 16

"But you say, 'What is the bride?' The bride is the church. ...Then the church will be married to the Lord, and EVERYONE WHO WAS NOT AFFILIATED WITH THE LORD'S CHURCH ON THIS EARTH WILL BE ON THE SIDELINES AT *THE WEDDING.*" [Emphasis added]

Wayne Cox, *The Church* (Liberal, Kansas: Wilderness Voice Publications) 3-4,16

Have you had enough? Do you understand their position yet?

A Brider believes the bride of Jesus Christ is the local Baptist Church. If you are not a member of a local independent Baptist church then you are not a part of the Bride of Jesus Christ. Did you get the part about the Baptists being the only faith and practice true to the scriptures? Basically the Baptist Briders are a group of high-minded people who don't know what they are talking about. A Brider believes that he is right and everybody else is wrong, and because of this the Lord is going to give him a special position throughout all eternity as the bride of Christ.

Some even go so far as to say that John Wesley, D. L. Moody, Martin Luther, etc., who, according to them, are not in the Bride because they were not in a scriptural New Testament Baptist church, will serve at the marriage supper of the Lamb. I was talking to a pastor one time and the subject of briderism came up. I asked him if D.L. Moody was in the bride of Christ, and he said, "No." Astounded at his answer I then asked him if Billy Sunday was in the bride of Christ, to which he answered again, "No." Both of these men were mightily used of God in their time, but were in the Congregational Church, and therefore, to a Brider, were not in the bride of Jesus Christ.

Baptist Briderism also teaches that the true church originated with John the Baptist, and there has been an unbroken line of Baptists down through the ages since John.

They believe that this is the only true church that Jesus Christ was referring to in Matt. 16:18: *"I will build my church and the gates of Hell shall not prevail against it."* They believe that this is a reference to the LOCAL INDEPENDENT BAPTIST CHURCH ONLY! And, as such, in their doctrine, the local independent Baptist Church is the only church with the AUTHORITY to baptize believers, send out missionaries, and do the work of the Lord. To them, God only works through the local church and that local church must be a Bible-believing independent Baptist church.

(I have always thought this strange since the Bible they "believe" and use is a King James 1611, and it did not come about through the local church. As a matter of fact, not one Baptist had anything to do with the word of God. Isn't that strange?)

They have what is called a FIXATION. Whenever they see the word CHURCH in the Bible, except for Acts 7:38, *"this is he, that was in the church in the wilderness,"* (although some may even believe that is a Baptist church also), they think BAPTIST. It's a Baptist fixation.

It's the same type of problem that the Church of Christ has when they see the word, "BAPTIZE" -they think WATER. They think it is always a reference to water.

Many of the Baptist Briders, when they see the word "baptize" often believe it is a reference to water. Especially when it comes to 1 Corinthians 12:13, *"For by one Spirit are we all baptized into one body, whether we be Jews or Gentiles, whether we be bond or free; and have been all made to drink into one Spirit."* Even though there is no water found anywhere in the context of the passage. We will be discussing all of these points further in the book.

A Baptist Brider, when he comes to the word CHURCH, will think local independent Baptist church. It's a Baptist fixation, and it is heresy. We will get into all of these things in the next chapters, but look at Acts 20:28 and Ephesians 5:25.

If the Briders were right, then Jesus Christ only died for the local independent Baptist Church. This would be bordering on the Calvinistic heresy of limited atonement, which states Christ's blood was only shed for the elect or, in this case, the blood was only shed for the Baptist church. Wasn't the church purchased with the blood of Jesus Christ? (Acts 20:28). Then, according to the Brider doctrine, everybody who is not in a local Baptist church is not in the bride and the blood was not shed for them. In a tape by Dr. Jack Hyles, made in the early '90's, titled, "Let's Be Baptist", he states in reference to Acts 20:28 that Christ shed his blood for the local Baptist church.

The basic points of the Baptist Bride heresy are as follows:
1. The local independent Baptist church is the Bride

of Jesus Christ. Only members of a true local independent Baptist church will be married to Jesus Christ, thus making up the bride in eternity.

2. The Church started with John the Baptist.
3. The Baptist church is the true Biblical church referenced in Matt. 16:18, *"And I say also unto thee, That thou art Peter, and upon this rock I will build my church; and the gates of hell shall not prevail against it,"* and therefore is the only church with Biblical authority to do the work of the Lord.
4. The word "church" in the Bible is always a reference to a local body of Baptist believers.

As Dr. Ken Blue so aptly put it in his booklet, *Baptist Briders BOLONEY:*

> Page 15
> "The only existence of a Baptist Bride church is in the imagination of the Baptist Briders. They fancy themselves to be in possession of the keys to the kingdom. To them, this little kingdom is their Baptist Bride church. The key is their baptism. See how it works? If you want to be in the bride of Christ, you must go through the Baptist Bride denomination. We only have one further word to say to all this Baptist Bride bologna - NUTS!"
> Dr. Ken Blue, *Baptist Briders Boloney* (Port Orchard, Washington, Local Church Publishing, 1997) 15

PRACTICAL BRIDERS OR BRIDERS IN PRACTICE

The Heresy: In Their Own Words

What I have printed so far, except for Dr. Blue, are quotes from, what I would term pure Briders. Those who believe only members of true Baptist churches will be in the bride in eternity. But there is another group of Briders that is much more prevalent, and they are what I call, the PRACTICAL BRIDERS. This group when confronted with the question, "Are you a Baptist Brider?" will emphatically answer, "No!" And in their own mind, they do not believe they are a Brider. The reason for this is they believe that at the rapture, all believers will make up the church, since after the rapture all believers will be called out and ASSEMBLED, and then all the saved will be in the bride.

They say they are not a Brider, BUT IN PRACTICE PREACH AND TEACH LIKE ONE BECAUSE ALL BELIEVERS ARE NOT IN THE BRIDE...YET. This is the stand of Dr. Jack Hyles, and many other Fundamentalists.

In the "1997/98 Catalogue from Golden State Baptist College," it states in their doctrinal statement under the Church:

> Page 17
> "We believe that the local church, which is the body and the espoused bride of Christ, is solely made up of born-again persons. (1 Corinthians 12:12-14;
> II Corinthians 11:2; Ephesians 1:22-23; 5:25-27)"
> *"Golden State Baptist College Handbook,"* (Santa Clara California, 1997-98) 17

31

The thing to notice here is that they state their belief that the local church is the espoused bride of Christ. Again in Roy Mason's book, *The Myth of the Universal Invisible Church E-x-p-l-o-d-e-d*, he states:

> "Louis Entzminger wrote a splendid book on the New Testament Church in which he took exactly the position that I have tried to set forth in the preceding pages. ...He said that a few Baptist preachers seemed to hold that the Bride would be composed of all of the saved that have held the essential doctrines of Baptists through the centuries. But, said he, he had concluded that the Bride will be composed of all of the saved."
>
> Roy Mason, *The Myth of the Universal Invisible Church E-x-p-l-o-d-e-d*, (Little Rock, Arkansas: Challenge Press, 1978) 79,72

So Mr. Entzminger lived, taught, and preached as a Brider in practice, but believed all the saved would be in the bride at the marriage. He was a Brider in practice.

In his book, *The Church*, Dr. Jack Hyles, states:

> Page 155
> "All believers are members of his family, but all believers are not members of the church. You must join a church to be a member of a local body. The church is His body, so all believers are not in His body. All believers are not in the church, and all believers are not in His body. When Jesus comes again, at the rapture all

believers will be called out and will assemble in Heaven. All believers will then become members of the church, because then we will all be a called out assembly. That called-out assembly, or church, will become his bride, but this does not happen until the rapture."

Page 71

"All believers have not yet been called out and assembled. They will not be assembled until the rapture when the church of the firstborn will be assembled in Heaven and all believers become a church. All believers are not now a church."

Page 72

"If anything refutes the invisible church, this is it. Jesus compares Himself and His church to a man and wife. Consequently, if there (Sic) an invisible church, then a man has an invisible wife. Jesus does not love an invisible church. He could have chosen another relationship to compare it with. He could have chosen angels because they are invisible to us. He could have used spirits or souls, but He chose to use the visibility of a man and his wife. Jesus is talking about a visible organization which is His church and His body."

Page 129

"Some men teach what we call the doctrine of the Baptist Bride. They believe that the only people who will be a part of the bride at the marriage of the Lamb will be Baptists, and all other saved people will merely be wedding

Here Comes The Bride

guests. Of course, that is not true. These people get the body mixed up with the bride. The bride will not be a bride until we get there, so it will include all believers. The future church will be the bride. The present church is not the bride; it is the body."

Dr. Jack Hyles, *The Church*, (Hammond, Indiana: Hyles - Anderson Publishers) 155,71-72,129

That position is the Brider in practice position. It is a political position. By this I mean that when asked, he can say that he is not a Baptist Brider, but in practice he is no different than a true Baptist Brider.

A BRIEF NOTE OF MORE HERESY

There is a note that I must make in regards to this book by Dr. Hyles. This does not have to do with the Baptist bride doctrine, but it does have to do with the deity of Jesus Christ. Since it was such an unscriptural statement, I thought I should mention it here. Dr. Hyles states in his book on the church, which was transcribed from Wednesday evening lessons given at the First Baptist Church in Hammond Indiana:

> Page 127
> "Did Jesus need to go to church? Absolutely. The Bible says He emptied himself of deity and became *a man. He did what He did, not as God, but as man.* [Emphasis added] Otherwise, He

could not have been our pattern. Jesus needed to go to church because He was a man. It was not to keep him from sinning, but for encouragement and fellowship, the same reasons we need to go to church."

This is complete and total heresy. Dr. Hyles has just said that Jesus was not God in the flesh. Where does the Bible say that Jesus "EMPTIED HIMSELF OF DEITY"? It's not there, at least not in a King James 1611 Authorized Version. Maybe the bible that Dr. Hyles has been studying says this, for this does appear in a New American Standard Version in Phillipians 2:7 which reads, "but emptied Himself". It must only be a coincidence that his statement agrees with the NASV.

There is a heresy known as Doceticism, which teaches that God left Jesus when he was on the cross, and that is the teaching found in the NASV in Luke 23:42. In the King James 1611 it reads, *"And he said unto Jesus, Lord, remember me when thou comest into thy kingdom."* But in the New American Standard Version it has been changed to "Jesus remember me." Lord has been changed to Jesus, thus leaving a mere man that bled and died on the cross.

Dr. Hyles has gone further than Doceticism, in that he has made our Lord a mere man, emptied of deity, all the time that he was on this earth. This is obvious heresy. First Timothy 3:16, *"And without controversy great is the mystery of godliness: GOD WAS MANIFEST IN THE FLESH..."* My Bible says that Jesus was God, but maybe Dr. Hyles bible doesn't say that, for the NASV takes God out of 1 Tim. 3:16.

Here Comes The Bride

In any case, what he has printed in this book is complete and total false doctrine; even a Jehovah's Witness would object to this. "HE DID WHAT HE DID, NOT AS GOD, BUT AS MAN" (page 127). Then the conclusion is that it was just a man who died on the cross for your sins.

You say, "but Dr. Hyles doesn't believe that." I have it here in print. If he doesn't believe that then where were the proofreaders, or editors who could have brought it to his attention, if this was a misprint? In the front of the book he says to have mercy on him as you read the book. With a heretical statement like that it must be mentioned and rebuked.

CHAPTER 2

THE STANDING AND STATE OF THE BELIEVER

It was during my first year of Bible school. I had been saved just two years prior and came from a background of absolutely no religion of any kind in our home. So many things were new to me, but I knew I was saved and Jesus Christ had changed me and made me a new creature in him. I knew that all I had done was to call on the name of my Savior and that he had saved me and given me a home in Heaven and a reason to live.

One day some Mormon missionaries came by the trailer to talk to some of us Bible students. There were about three of us, and we listened to their false gospel. We then started a discussion, in hopes of persuading them that they were wrong. For me it was also a chance to learn what they really believed, since at the time I didn't know.

Here Comes The Bride

After quite a bit of time had passed and out of frustration with the way things were going I spoke up and said, "I'd like to give my testimony of how I got saved." With a look of impatience, the Mormons agreed and I proceeded to tell how I got saved. With tears in my eyes, I told how the Lord had come into my heart, and I was now saved and on my way to Heaven.

I never will forget their response. They said, "That's good, but there is so much more that you can have. You're missing out on all that God wants for you." Inside I got mad. They were telling me that Jesus wasn't enough, that my salvation was imperfect and I needed to do something to make it perfect. I was furious at that, though I kept my testimony and didn't lose my temper, I never will forget that day. I knew that Jesus had given me a perfect salvation that could not be improved upon.

The same thing could be said for the heresy of the Baptist bride doctrine. They believe that a person is saved by grace through faith. Oh, yes, the blood of Jesus Christ cleanseth us from all sin. *"For whosoever shall call upon the name of the Lord shall be saved."* Romans 10:13. Jesus paid it all, etc..

But according to a Brider you can change your eternal position in Heaven by joining a proper Baptist church. Now think about that for a minute. That's works, plain and simple. And one of the works needed to be at the zenith of your salvation is to be baptized into a local Baptist church. AN ETERNAL POSITION HAS BEEN NOW PLACED INTO THE HANDS OF SINNERS. Oh, but they're saved sinners. I'm talking about the pastors of these churches.

They now, according to the Briders, have the power to determine if someone can be in the bride or not. Can a pastor kick someone out of a church if he believes he should? Can a pastor refuse to accept a member if he believes he should? Aren't pastors sinners like you and me? I'm sure there has been many a person kicked out of a church just because they didn't believe everything that the pastor believed. Does that mean they got kicked out of the bride of Christ and they will not be in the bride in eternity? In the Brider doctrine it does.

Think about it. In their belief, a position in eternity is relegated and determined by the local church. If there is no Baptist church in your area to go to then you are not in the bride. If the Baptist church in your area stinks and there is a biblical Bible church close by then that's not good enough. You're not in the bride.

What they have done is added to your salvation. Your salvation, according to them, is not complete until you are a member of a local independent Baptist church. Oh, they will say that it is complete. But what they really believe is that your eternal position is not perfected until you are a member of a true local independent Baptist church.

Those who believe and adhere to the Brider teaching are extremely heady and high-minded. It is a better than thou position much like the Pharisees of the New Testament.

To think that I could improve upon what my Lord and Savior has done for me is to take the glory from Jesus Christ. *"For by grace are ye saved through faith; and that not of yourselves: it is the gift of God: not of works,*

Here Comes The Bride

LEST ANY MAN SHOULD BOAST" (Ephesians 2:8-9).

I've heard them boast already in chapter 1, saying that the Baptist church is the true church, the pure church, etc. It's enough to make a sow puke. Yes, I'm a Baptist. I believe, as a whole, they are the most Biblical group, and I agree with the distinctives, but to say that because of my belief after salvation, I am going to have a higher position in Glory is to add works to the grace of God in the day and age in which we live.

It is a slap in the face of Jesus Christ and what He did for us on the cross!!!

Now there are a number of things that happen to you when you receive Jesus Christ into your heart according to John 1:12, *"But as many as received him, to them gave he power to become the sons of God, even to them that believe on his name."* These are things the Lord does, either himself or the Holy Spirit, for even the Holy Spirit is called *"The Lord"* in 2 Corinthians 3:17.

The changes that take place in you or in your destiny have to do with your standing in Jesus Christ. When you get saved your standing is unchangeable. You had nothing to do with them in the first place, except call on the Lord Jesus Christ and ask him to save you. He does the rest. He is the one that saved you and he is the one that did a number of other things. But it was all by grace.

Many unchangeable events happened when you got saved, they have to do with your standing, and I am going to cover some of them. To cover them all would take too long and this book would end up a book on theology, which is not the purpose.

As some of you, who are well schooled in the things of the word of God, come to this section, you may ask, "why is he going into all of this?" And I have no doubt that some of you will think this section is unrelated to the subject of Briderism. So please understand that my aim here is to the average church member in the average Baptist Bride church who has gotten years of pastoral authority preaching, but very little in the way of Bible; ESPECIALLY BIBLE DOCTRINE. So, please bear with me as we go into all of this.

I had one young Christian man, who was also young in the Lord, come to me for help on the Baptist Bride heresy. I went over some things in the Bible with him. And when he found out that I had a rough draft of this thesis, he asked if he could read it. I told him it was far from finished, but if he wanted to I would let him. So I gave it to him to read and he said it really cleared up some of the confusion that he had.

So please consider those who are sitting in church, and basically starving for some real Bible teaching and preaching, instead of brow beating and control. This will be a study of your standing and state in Christ Jesus. Many Briders do not know the difference between the two and consequently have them mixed up.

STANDING BEFORE SALVATION IN ADAM

1 Corinthians 15:22 "For as in Adam all die, even so in Christ shall all be made alive."

Here Comes The Bride

Before you were saved you were, IN Adam. That was how God saw you, and that is the biblical designation for all who are lost.

The first man is of the earth, and the earth will pass away one day.

DEAD

> Ephesians 2:1 "And you hath he quickened, who were dead in trespasses and sins;"

You were dead spiritually, dead in trespasses and sins. This is a spiritual designation. Obviously you were alive physically, but before God you were spiritually dead.

A few years ago, my grandmother died. Her body is buried in Modesto, California. She is no longer a part of my life, and I am no longer a part of her life. I don't know her any more. She is dead. So too, you were dead in trespasses and sins. God did not know you. You were not a part of his life, and He was not a part of your life, because you were dead.

It doesn't matter how religious you are, or were. Your standing was the same, you were dead in trespasses and sins.

A CHILD OF WRATH

> Ephesians 2:3 "...and were by nature the children of wrath, even as others."
>
> John 3:36"...he that believeth not the Son shall not see life; but the wrath of God abideth on him."

The wrath of God had not yet fallen upon you, for God is merciful and longsuffering, not willing that any should perish. But that wrath was getting ever closer with each passing second of time that you lived, lost and without salvation in the Lord Jesus Christ.

NO HOPE AND WITHOUT GOD

> Ephesians 2:12 "That at that time ye were without Christ, being aliens from the commonwealth of Israel, and strangers from the covenants of promise, having no hope, and without God in the world."

The verse speaks for itself. But before you received Jesus Christ, you were without God, without Christ, and without hope.

A CHILD OF THE DEVIL

> John 8:44 "Ye are of your father the devil." Ephesians 2:2 "Wherein time past ye walked according to the course of this world, according to the prince of the power of the air, the sprit that now worketh in the children of disobedience:"

You had the wrong father! The Devil was your father.

And he is the father of all who are not saved. That was your standing before you asked Jesus Christ to come into your heart and become your personal Savior. There was nothing that you could do to change your standing in Adam. The only way that it

Here Comes The Bride

could be changed was to get saved because you were lost. You needed a new birth (Jn. 3) because your first birth was earthy. (1 Cor. 15:47-49) And with that first birth came the wrong father, the Devil.

Praise the Lord though! There was a day when you realized that you were a lost sinner and you needed to be saved. You heard the old, old story of Jesus and his love- how he went to an old rugged cross, suffered, bled and died to pay for your sins. Then you prayed and asked Jesus to forgive you of your sins and to come into your heart and be your personal Savior. Oh, what a friend! I've found a friend and such a friend! He loved me 'er I knew him. What a friend we have in Jesus! All our sins and griefs to bear. What a privilege to carry, Everything to God in prayer.

There was a change that took place. It was as if you had started over. A new life had begun and truly you did have a new life. Old things were passed away and all things were made new. Thank the Lord Jesus Christ for his marvelous grace.

But what all happened to you when you got saved? What did the Lord do when you received him into your heart? And the key to that last statement is: THE LORD. He is the one that has done it all.

YOUR STANDING AFTER SALVATION

BORN AGAIN

1 Peter 1:23 "Being born again, not of corruptible seed, but of incorruptible, by the

word of God, which liveth and abideth for ever."

John 3:3 "Jesus answered and said unto him, Verily, verily, I say unto thee, Except a man be born again, he cannot see the kingdom of God."

If you have come to the Lord Jesus Christ, and have received him into your heart, then you have been born again. Anything short of receiving Jesus Christ into your heart is not salvation and therefore no new birth has taken place. "But as many as have received him, to them gave he power to become the sons of God." John 1:12. If you have received the Lord, then you are born again.

Before you received the Lord you were spiritually dead. You had a dead spirit. If you are saved, you now are spiritually alive. You have been spiritually born again. This happened when you got saved, and there is nothing that you can do after you are saved to change it. I doubt that anybody ever has wanted to change it, but if they did it is an unalterable spiritual condition. Praise God!

IN CHRIST

1 Corinthians 15:22 "For as in Adam all die, even so in Christ shall all be made alive. Ephesians 2:13 But now IN CHRIST JESUS ye who sometimes were far off are made nigh by the blood of Christ."

Here Comes The Bride

This is a very important doctrine to understand and believe. You are NOW, IN CHRIST according to the word of God.

As we mentioned earlier, before you got saved you were in Adam. That was your condition designated by the word of God. Now you are in Jesus Christ.

You did not get in Christ when you joined the Baptist Church. You got in Christ when you got saved, by receiving Jesus Christ into your heart. There was a two-fold exchange that took place. You were put in Christ and Jesus Christ came into you. Colossians 1:27 " ...*which is Christ in you, the hope of glory:*".

This truth opens up many things about a Christian's salvation in the word of God. For example, Galatians 2:20 *"I am crucified with Christ..."* If you are in him, then you are considered crucified with him. Your flesh spiritually has already been crucified. You are a walking dead man. *"To the one we are the savour of death unto death;..."* (2 Corinthians 2:16). To the lost you stink.

Another point to consider: If you are in Christ, then you have already been resurrected and are already seated in heavenly places in Christ Jesus. *"And hath raised us up together, and made us sit together in heavenly places in Christ Jesus:"* Ephesians 2:6. You are seated in Heaven because you are IN HIM. And since he is in Heaven then you are also, spiritually. To those of you who think that you can lose your salvation and then get it back, you need to think about that and get hold of it.

One more thing that I want to bring out about your being in Christ is Colossians 2:10. The reason I want to mention it is because it shows that you are complete in Jesus Christ. Colossians 2:10 says, *"And ye are complete in him, which is the head of all principality and power."*

A Brider says that you are not complete until you get in a local independent Baptist church. For, according to them, you are not in the bride until you get in a local Baptist church, and therefore you are not complete, as far as your salvation goes. Of course, they go round and round about how you are completely saved, even if you are not in a local independent Baptist church, but who's kidding whom?

They mean that you are not going to Hell; that much of your salvation is complete. But they do not believe that you are complete in him. According to them, you are not complete in him until you get into his body, which, to them, is the local independent Baptist church and therefore you are in the bride.

However the word of God says you are complete in him. And if you are complete then you are complete and there is nothing that you can do to improve upon it.

The haughty Briders have taken a work of grace, which is being in the bride, and which is based on the death of the Lord Jesus Christ and his blood atonement for salvation. They have stolen that work of grace for their own glory. They have stolen the glory from the Lord Jesus Christ.

They stand in the pulpits, proclaim that their church is the bride of Christ, that you must join their church in order to be in the bride, and then they glory in that falsely. Instead of giving the Lord ALL of the glory they steal it from him and try to direct it towards themselves. According to them, a person can now earn a higher position in Heaven by joining their church through the baptismal waters.

The Bible says that you are complete in him!!! You cannot add to your position. Your position, as well as your salvation, is complete in Jesus Christ. He is to get all of the glory.

JUSTIFIED

"Much more then, being now justified by his blood, we shall be saved from wrath through him" (Romans 5:9).

To be justified means to be declared righteous in a legal sense. Strong's Concordance says, "accounting the guilty just before God." Think about it. God has declared you righteous. You will never have to stand and give an account of your sins at the White Throne Judgement. God has judiciously declared you without sin on the basis of the blood of Jesus Christ.

A few years ago we had a big court case out in California. The case had captured the attention of much of the whole world. And the question that seemed to be on everybody's mind was, "Would O.J. Simpson be found guilty or innocent?" He had been arrested for the murder of Ron Goldman and Nicole Simpson.

After the criminal trial he was tried in a civil court and found to be guilty of the crime. When they asked the jurors if there was any doubt as to his innocence they replied, "None whatsoever." But at the time of the criminal case we had no idea if he would be found guilty or innocent.

The day finally came and the verdict was read. The head of the jury stood up and said, "Your Honor. We find Ornithal James Simpson, not guilty in the murder of Ronald Goldman, and not guilty in the murder of Nicole Simpson." But he was guilty. That day as I watched the proceedings, I watched O.J. Simpson walk out of that courtroom...JUSTIFIED! - Just as if he had not committed the crime.

In your standing before God you are justified, if you are saved. But if the brider heresy were true, then those who are not in the true Baptist church are less justified than those who are in the true Baptist church. Their belief affects their standing. There is no scriptural way this could be true. There was a day, when I walked out justified: Just as if I had never sinned against the holy God. I have been justified, and so have you if you are saved, regardless of the denomination to which you belong.

SANCTIFIED

> 1 Corinthians 6:11 "And such were some of you: but ye are washed, but ye are sanctified, but ye are justified in the name of the Lord Jesus, and by the Spirit of our God."

Every saved person has been set apart from this world, by the Spirit of our God, when they got saved. Before you were saved you were a part of the world and you were a child of wrath even as others. God only sees two groups of people - the saved and the lost. The lost are under the wrath of God (John 3:36 "...he that believeth not the Son shall not see life; but the *wrath of God abideth on him."*) and are part of the world. But the saved have been sanctified, that is they have been set apart from this world unto God.

When God looks at the lost souls in this world he sees a soul that is unholy, sinful and part of a corrupted sinful world. When he looks at a saved person he sees them through the blood of his Son and he sees a soul that has been clothed in the righteousness of his Son. That soul is set apart from this corrupt world and as such is SANCTIFIED.

Webster's definition of sanctify: "To make holy; to set apart as holy; consecrate." Therefore, it is a part of the Heavenly world, and that will never change. If you hear some preacher saying that a certain church is not separated and therefore you are not in the bride because you are not separated, you can tell them that the Lord separated you when you got saved for he sanctified you.

A common point that the Briders will make is that the word church means: called out assembly. To teach this they go to the Greek word for Church, which is ekklesia. The Greek word "ek" means, out of. The root word of ekklesia is Kaleo, which means to call. When they add the word "assembly" to the definition it is not in the Greek word. It could be used, but you could also say it means a called out one, or a called out group. It is not absolute to be defined as, "assembly."

The Briders say that word church means called out assembly, thus making the independent Baptists the true church, since they are the only church that has been separated from Roman Catholicism, were never a part of that church, and they were never started by a man. You cannot trace the Baptist church back to a man. Therefore the Baptist church is the only true called out assembly. Wrong!

While many of those facts are true, they have nothing to do with your spiritual standing. Every person that has ever been born again has been called out of this world and sanctified when they got saved. They have been set apart from this world by Jesus Christ and as such are part of the called out assembly, which is the church of God.

In your daily walk with the Lord, yes, you need to be separated from the world (2 Corinthians 6:14-17), but this gets into our state, which I will get to in a few pages.

Right now, all of these things have happened to every person that has been saved and it will never change. I know that I am repeating myself, but the thickheaded Pharisees have a hard time understanding correct Bible doctrine.

REDEEMED

> Colossians 1:14, *"In whom we have redemption through his blood, even the forgiveness of sins:"*

Microsoft's dictionary has the following for the first definition of Redeem, "to make something acceptable or pleasant in spite of its negative qualities or aspects." The blood of the Lamb has made you acceptable and pleasant to God. It was the blood of Jesus Christ that paid for your sins. The debt that you could never pay was paid in full making you acceptable with God.

REGENERATED

> Titus 3:5, "Not by works of righteousness which we have done, but according to his mercy he saved us, by the washing of regeneration, and renewing of the Holy Ghost;"

To be regenerated is to have new life put into you. When a battery goes dead it needs to be recharged, or you could say, it needs to be "regenerated." It is brought back to life.

It is an imperfect illustration though in this respect. Before you were born again, you had no spiritual life in you. As a baby you're innocent, but you were not regenerated. As you came to the knowledge of sin, then you lost your innocence.

When you were saved you were regenerated as you were washed in the blood of the Lamb. You now have life, eternal life, whereas before you were dead. Just like a dead battery.

SEALED BY THE HOLY SPIRIT

> Ephesians 4:30, "And grieve not the holy Spirit of God, whereby ye are sealed unto the day of redemption."

You will be protected from corruption spiritually until the day you leave this world, because when you were saved the Holy Spirit sealed you. This is explained more when you get to Spiritual Circumcision.

IMPUTED RIGHTEOUSNESS

2 Corinthians 5:21, "For he hath made him to be sin for us, who knew no sin; that we might be made the righteousness of God in him."

Your sins were placed on Jesus and not only that, but Jesus Christ became sin for you. God's righteousness was placed or imputed to you when God saved you. When God looks at a born again person he sees the righteousness of his Son, Jesus Christ. And that standing will never change.

A SON OF GOD

John 1:12, "But as many as received him, to them gave he power to become the sons of God, even to them that believe on his name:"
1 John 3:2 "Beloved, now are we the sons of God..."

You have been born and are now one of his sons. Before you were saved, Satan was your father, now the Lord is your father.

If you are a woman, once you are born again, then you spiritually are a son of God. This is your spiritual classification.

SPIRITUALLY CIRCUMCISED

Colossians 2:11, "In whom (notice that, you are in him) also ye are circumcised with the circumcision made without hands, in the putting off the body of the sins of the flesh by the circumcision of Christ:"

Your body of flesh has been "put off" or in other words cut loose from your soul. This was done by the word of God (Hebrews 4:12) when you got saved. Your soul is now loose from your body and has been sealed by the Holy Spirit. You will now stay clean and pure until you go to be with the Lord.

It's like when fruit is preserved in jars. After the lids have sealed the jar, the fruit inside stays pure, though the outside of the jar may get dusty and dirty on the shelf in the pantry.

If you are saved then your soul is preserved unto the Heavenly Kingdom, but the flesh, the outside, is dirty (Romans 7:18-24) and needs to be crucified daily. The soul on the inside has been cut loose from the flesh, sealed by the Holy Spirit. So your soul now stays clean, even though your flesh is dirty.

ADOPTED

Galatians 4:4-5b, 7b, "But when the fullness of the time was come, God sent forth his Son, made of a woman, made under the law, to redeem them that were under the law, (5b)... that we might receive the adoption of sons. (7b)...and if a son, then an heir of God through Christ."

You are now a joint heir with Jesus Christ (Romans 8:17).

There are many more verses that deal with our standing in Jesus Christ. For the sake of space and due to the fact that this is not a study in theology, I am going to cut it short on ALL of the doctrines that have to do with our standing as a Christian.

The following truths on a Christian's standing are essential to the understanding of where the Baptist Briders get scripturally messed up. Keep in mind that all of these things that we are covering happen to a Christian, any Christian, regardless of church denomination at the time that they get born again. These things are done by the Lord to the sinner, and the sinner has done nothing but receive Jesus Christ into his heart.

The following verse is the kingpin, so to speak, on showing where the Briders are unscriptural. Consequently, they have a time with this verse and will often go to the Greek to make it say something that it doesn't say. Not all will go to the Greek, yet all will say it means something other than what it says.

BAPTIZED INTO THE BODY OF JESUS CHRIST

1 Corinthians 12:13, "For by one Spirit are we all baptized into one body, whether we be Jews or Gentiles, whether we be bond or free; and have been all made to drink into one Spirit."

When you get saved you get in Christ. A Brider will say that you can be "in Christ" but not in "his body." They have to say that in order for their heresy to work. Notice what the Bible said, not what it means, but what it said. You have to watch out for some one who will tell you what the Bible means. It says what it means and means what it says. The problem is to believe what it says as it says it.

It says, *"by one Spirit,"* which is the Holy Spirit, by that Spirit. Not by a man who has been enabled by the Spirit. It says, *"by one Spirit."* If it says that it is by the Spirit then I believe that it is by the Spirit. The Holy Spirit Baptizes, (which is immersion- notice the word, "into") the believer at the time of salvation into one, one, one, one, one body. And after that you are in Christ. And that will never change. This is not a preacher, who has been enabled by the Holy Spirit, baptizing someone into the local church. WHY? Because it doesn't say that! Briders will say it means that, but they are about as cuckoo as a cuckoo clock. If it were a local independent Baptist church body, then you would not have one body, but many bodies.

When the body of Christ is spoken of in the Bible

it is always spoken of in the singular, and never in the plural.

By the way, you cannot say, "the local independent Baptist church is the bride of Christ." Why? Because the logical response would be, "which one?" If they are all independent then there would have to be a certain one that the Bible is referring to. If it could refer to any of them then you do not end up with a bride, but many brides of Christ.

As one Brider said when responding to this point, "there are many one bodies." What? Many one bodies? This is what happens to a man when he is too proud to admit that what he believes is not scriptural. He starts talking like an idiot.

Now the common point that the Brider will try to make about this text is that it was written to the local church, the church at Corinth. And therefore the context is the local church and it would be taken out of context if you were to apply this verse to all of the saved regardless of church affiliation.

Well, I thought that I would check at the beginning of the epistle to see if they were right. 1 Corinthians 1:2 reads, *"Unto the church of God which is at Corinth, to them that are sanctified in Christ Jesus,* (Do you remember what I said about being sanctified? Every saved person is sanctified at the point of salvation, so this epistle is written to all the saved. You say, "All of the saved in Corinth were in the church which was at Corinth." That's an assumption but I'll give it to you for now.)

Called to be saints, WITH ALL THAT IN EVERY PLACE CALL UPON THE NAME OF JESUS CHRIST

OUR LORD, BOTH THEIRS AND OURS" (emphasis added).

Isn't it amazing how the Bible clears things up for you? It is obvious that these "air head" preachers can't read their own Bibles.

Not only was this epistle written to the saints at Corinth, but also to ALL THAT IN EVERY PLACE CALL UPON JESUS CHRIST. Now I believe that "all" means "all". And I believe that "every place" means "every place". THEY DON'T!!! They are blind guides who are perverting the truth of the word of God. So the epistle to the Corinthians was written to all of the saints in every place. Though it was written to the local church at Corinth, it was not limited in its address to the local church at Corinth. What is so hard about that? What is so hard about it, is that it doesn't fit into their private interpretation, so they have to lie in order to teach their heresy.

BECOME PART OF THE BODY OF JESUS CHRIST

1 Corinthians 12:27, "Now ye are the body of Christ, and members in particular." Ephesians 5:30, "For we are members of his body, of his flesh, and of his bones."

You are part of Jesus Christ. You say, "I don't understand that." But that is what the Bible says, so believe it. You are a member of his body. When you are baptized into Jesus Christ you not only are placed in him, but you become part of him.

Jesus prayed in John 17:21, *"That they all may be one; as thou, Father, art in me, and I in thee, that they also may be one in us:"* and 1 Corinthians 6:15 reads, *"Know ye not that your bodies are the members of Christ? shall I then take the members of Christ, and make them the members of an harlot? God forbid."*

We say that when a person gets in an accident and loses an arm or a leg that they have been dismembered. They are missing a part or member of their body. When you get saved you become a member of Jesus Christ's body of bone and flesh (Eph. 5:30). A Brider when he sees the word "BODY," in 1 Corinthians 12:27, thinks local body of believers. But, you see, he does that because he has a mental fixation. *"Now ye are the body of Christ."* He is thinking of the local independent Baptist church. But that is not what it says.

The problem is that the average independent fundamental Baptist Brider has a problem believing the word of God as it is written. It's a heart matter. Furthermore, if his heresy is destroyed by the scriptures, then he can no longer manipulate and pressure his people into serving "the church." (See Chapter one sermon excerpt of Dr. Thomas Cassidy, where he is stressing that his people must be faithful to the church.) No, you must be faithful to the Lord Jesus Christ! The average Brider, in all practicality, will substitute his church for God.

In regards to a Christian being part of the body of Jesus Christ, let's look at one of the greatest scriptures on eternal security in the Bible. 2 Timothy 2:13, *"If we believe not, yet he abideth faithful: he cannot deny himself."*

Notice that Paul includes himself with Timothy, "we." It is possible for a Christian to get so backslidden as to deny that he has ever been saved. This is common when a Christian gets mad at God. For example Simon Peter, when he denied the Lord, was mad at the Lord for not letting him fight. The third time he denies the Lord he curses and swears. And if you had been there and did not know him, you never would have thought that he was a disciple of Jesus Christ.

So too, there are saved people who for one reason or another have gotten mad at God and denied that there even is a God. Are they still saved? According to this verse they are. If you are saved, you are part of his body, and therefore you may deny him but "HE CANNOT DENY HIMSELF."

> John 10:27-29, "My sheep hear my voice, and I know them, and they follow me: And I give unto them eternal life; and they shall never perish, neither shall any man pluck them out of my hand. My Father, which gave them me, is greater than all; and no man is able to pluck them out of my Father's hand."

I've used this many a time to show someone they are eternally secure. Spiritually it makes an excellent application, but doctrinally it does not apply. You see it's one thing to be in his hand. It's another thing to be part of the hand. Do you see the difference? And that position or standing takes place by grace when you are saved and will never change. It happens to every born again believer that has ever been and will ever be until the Rapture, not just the independent Baptists.

    These doctrines are events that take place at the time a person accepts Jesus Christ as their personal Savior. They happen to all who accept him and not just the Baptists.

    One more time, these have to do with your standing, and your standing is dependent upon Jesus Christ, not you. Your standing will never change regardless of what you do after you have been saved. Works will never affect your standing in Jesus Christ. Your standing has been set by the word of God, which is settled in Heaven. Amen and Amen!!!

Here Comes The Bride

CHAPTER 3

YOUR STATE

Unlike your standing, which is unchangeable, your state does change as you go through this life. Your state is your spiritual condition in relation to your walk with the Lord on a fellowship basis. Are you in fellowship with him? Are there sins in your life that have grieved Him and quenched your fellowship with him? Your spiritual condition changes from time to time.

Often you will go through more than one state in a single day. You may start a day out in fellowship with God and something comes up during the day, which causes you to sin against the Lord, and your fellowship with Him gets broken. So you go to the Lord in prayer, confess it to Him and get back in fellowship with Him. You have just been in two states, in fellowship with the Lord and out of fellowship with the Lord. The state that you are in at any given time is dependent on a variety of things, such as: how long you have been saved, if you are fighting the Lord, if you are discouraged, offended, mad, glad, prayerful and so on.

I will say that the majority of what kind of state you are in depends on you and your love for the Lord Jesus Christ. Your love for him will motivate you to choose the right things, such as reading your bible, prayer, church and telling others about the Lord, thus bringing about a spiritual state in you.

It is your lack of love for him that will cause you to choose those things that will gratify self, such as overeating, laziness, anger, vengeance, etc. (Galatians 5 has a list of these things.) You end up carnal, or stay a baby spiritually.

Now some, not all, of the Bible is written with regards to your standing. And some, not all, of the Bible is written with regards to your state. And most of the Bible is written with regards to things other than both of these.

The Bible has parts written to Jews, Gentiles, and the church of God. Most of the word of God has to do with a kingdom on this earth and the second coming of the Lord Jesus Christ, when he comes back and sets up that kingdom on this earth. There are far more references to the second coming of the Lord Jesus Christ than there are to the first coming of the Lord Jesus Christ.

There are also different dispensations, or periods of time, in the Bible, that apply to that specific time. Hence, the Bible is an infinite book written and preserved by God in the King James Version of 1611, and has divisions in it. A heresy is when part of the word of God is applied in the wrong way. 2 Timothy 2:15 says, *"Study to shew thyself approved unto God, a workman that needeth not to be ashamed, rightly dividing the word of truth."* There is a biblical division in the scriptures between your standing and your state. The problem comes up when you don't make that division between the two and start applying verses wrongly. In other words, verses about your state that you apply to your standing and vice versa. The Briders will often do this.

For example: 2 Corinthians 5:17, *"Therefore if any man be in Christ, he is a new creature: old things are passed away; behold, all things are become new."* This verse has nothing to do with your state, or the way that you are living. It is a statement on your standing and is true of all believers.

I've heard preachers use this verse in reference to a Christian's state. I've heard them say that if a Christian is saved then he will not do the things that he used to, and if he did do the things that he used to do then he was never saved. They then quote the verse, *"If any man be in Christ he is a new creature: old things are passed away; behold all things are become new."*

This would then cause young Christians, or Christians that were weak in the faith, to doubt their salvation because they were still fighting sins that they had before they were saved. Or, maybe, they weren't even fighting the sins anymore, but out of discouragement, just living with them.

Now, there is no excuse biblically for sin in your life. There will be no alibi when we stand before the

Lord that will justify our sins. However I'm sure there has been many a saved man or woman that tried to quit smoking and has become discouraged and given up trying. Along comes some preacher and says that if you are saved you are a new creature in Christ. Therefore you won't continue in those old sins, and if you are continuing in those old sins then you had better check your salvation.

The saved man or woman thinks, "Well I guess I didn't get saved," and they go get "saved" all over again, thinking that now they will get the victory over their smoking. They get baptized again, and yet the desire to smoke is still there.

I wonder how many have ended up scared to death, thinking that maybe somewhere sometime they committed the unpardonable sin, and now they can't get saved. (Biblically the unpardonable sin is impossible to commit in the day and age in which we live, when you study and find out what it is.)

Some of you may think I'm being extreme. You'd be surprised what goes on in independent Baptist churches that have about as much Bible knowledge as the graduates of the daily Vacation Bible School do! It's a disgrace what some preachers have put some Christians through.

I am not writing this thinking I'm perfect and have everything 100% correct. But I've seen common saints, who may not be spiritual giants and all that stuff. I've seen them get so discouraged due to a preacher grinding them into the ground because in the preacher's opinion, they do not meet all of his requirements for a "saved person." They get "lost and saved," two or three times because they have been pushed into thinking that if they are not living on a certain spiritual plane then they are not saved.

There has been many a common Christian who has suffered needlessly, due to the preacher in the pulpit putting them down, or making them feel guilty because they do not live up to what he thinks a Christian should be. He uses the verse, *"therefore if any man be in Christ, he is a new creature,"* as though that verse was referring to your daily walk.

A person that is saved has two natures, an old man and a new man. Ephesians 4:22, *"That ye put off concerning the former conversation the old man, which is corrupt according to the deceitful lusts; 23 And be renewed in the spirit of your mind; 24 And that ye put on the new man, which after God is created in righteousness and true holiness."*

Look at Romans 7:14-25 for an example of the two natures. Read it! I'm going to quote parts of it, but read the whole passage: (18) *For I know that in me (that is, in my flesh,) dwelleth no good thing: for to will is present with me; but how to perform that which is good I find not. (22) For I delight in the law of God after the INWARD MAN* (Emphasis added). In verse 18 Paul mentions the flesh and in verse 22 he mentions the inward man.

He has TWO NATURES OR PARTS: The old man, and the new man. The old man has no desire whatsoever to live for the Lord Jesus Christ. The new man does desire to live for the Lord, but he has a free will and he decides which desire he is going to fulfill. The more you live for Jesus Christ and reckon yourself dead to the old man, the more spiritual your state is and will become.

This is accomplished by spending much time in the Bible and prayer, while at the same time denying your flesh the pleasures of sin (you don't hear much about self denial in the churches nowadays. What's coming across the pulpits of America today is that God will give you whatever you desire).

A spiritual walk is one that is filled with self-denial, not self-fulfillment! Jesus said, *"Whosoever will come after me, let him deny himself, and take up his cross, and follow me"* (Mk 8:34b). What have you denied yourself lately? Have you put the Lord and his desires first? Read your Bible instead of watching television? Talk to the Lord in prayer instead of gossiping on the phone? Listen to preaching or clean gospel music instead of your fleshly music, which includes much of the modern "Christian" music? This is what is involved in determining what kind of state you are in.

A Christian is capable of doing anything and committing any act that a lost man is capable of doing or committing. The problem is that many of the so-called spiritual "elites" don't think this is possible. Let me give you an example.

I read about a saved man one time that was committing fornication. It did not bother him, or so it seemed. Not only did it not bother him, he told people about it at church where he was a member, and was not ashamed of the sin which he was committing. If that was not bad enough, the woman with whom he was fornicating was his father's wife.

Could this man be saved and do such a thing? But, *"if any man be in Christ, he is a new creature, old things are passed away; behold, all things are become new."* I can hear it now, "If this man were saved he couldn't live like that. He needs to be born again!" "He may think he's saved but I'll tell you he's headed straight for hell." This would be the cry from the average Brider pulpit that wrests the scriptures.

This man is found in your Bible in 1 Corinthians 5 and Paul commands the church in Corinth to kick him out. But in 2 Corinthians 2 Paul tells the church to forgive him and to confirm their love towards him.

This was a saved man and the whole time he was a new creature in Christ (Standing). He was living in open sin, and was not repenting of it or forsaking it, until being rebuked by Paul and the church.

He was in a carnal state, and was out of fellowship with God. Then he repented and got his heart and life right with God and was brought back in fellowship with the brethren and with God. His state changed, but his standing never did.

There are three main states that a Christian can be in, and a fourth that all saved people will be in when they reach Heaven. It may seem needless to cover these states here, but I believe there will be many things that apply to these heretics who are propagating the Baptist bride heresy.

The first of these states is that of a:

BABE IN CHRIST

> 1 Corinthians 3:1 "And I, brethren, could not speak unto you as unto spiritual, but as unto carnal, even as unto babes in Christ. (2) I have fed you with milk, and not with meat: for hitherto ye were not able to bear it, neither yet now are ye able."

Here Comes The Bride

A babe is, ideally, a new Christian who has recently been born again. Since they have just been BORN, spiritually, they are a babe. And babies have certain characteristics about them that mark them as babies.

Babies cry a lot. If they want something then they cry for it. Their request is always for their self. They are not concerned about any one else's needs. They are only concerned about their own needs. This is natural, for they are a babe.

Another thing that is characteristic of babies is that they can't take care of themselves. They need help. If a baby doesn't get the help that it needs then it will die.

It's a sad day in which we live to see and hear about babies that have been abandoned by their parents. The father generally is nowhere to be found. Then the mother gives birth and deserts the child. We had a case recently where a mother went out into a field and gave birth to a baby and left it there to die. That just kind of wrenches your heart when you hear about it. But a baby cannot survive if it is not taken care of.

Babies do a lot of eating and sleeping. They need to be fed. A new Christian needs to be fed from the word of God! And they need to be fed milk. Salvation, eternal security, prayer, the word of God, baptism, etc., nothing deep, just good old Bible to get them grounded and settled in their salvation. Babies are hungry. A new Christian ought to be hungry for the word of God.

When I got saved in 1977, there was a man who helped me greatly. Every night for a month we would have Bible study. And then every other night for the next month we had Bible study. At the time we didn't know that the A.V. 1611 was the inerrant word of God, but we studied and I grew in the Lord in those two months.

I never will forget what a joy it was to learn about the things of God. For the first time in my life I was getting answers to the questions that I had about this life. For years I had wondered what there was in this life that was worth living for, and I had not been able to come up with an answer. When I got saved and started reading and studying the Bible, I started to get answers to my life long questions. I was a babe in the Lord and I was HUNGRY.

There is a problem when a person gets saved and they don't grow in the Lord. Before I go any further, let me say this: There is no excuse for you not to grow in the Lord. You will not be able to stand before Jesus Christ and point your finger at someone and blame them for your spiritual condition. You will not be able to pass the buck. (See Genesis 3) But having said that, there are some bad situations that young Christians get into. One of which is having a pastor who has very little knowledge of the word of God. He spends his time teaching and preaching on attendance and giving. That is the average diet of many Independent Baptist churches in this day and age.

Attendance (that's, be here when the doors are open) and go soul winning. Now there is nothing wrong with that as long as it is in the proper perspective. There has got to be a BALANCE. Too much of anything will make you unbalanced, whether it is prayer, Bible study, soul winning, good works, etc. A newborn baby doesn't even know how to walk, let alone work. If you ride a horse too soon you'll make it a swayback that is good for nothing. I've seen new Christians sacrificed on the altar of church growth more than once. A Christian is a babe when they are first born again and they stay a babe for a good while. And what they need is to be fed a balanced diet. If they are not getting a balanced diet then they may get off track spiritually. If attendance and giving are the majority of their diet then they may never leave the "babe" state.

There have been Christians who have been babes in the Lord and have stayed that way until the day they went home to be with the Lord, even though they were saved for 40 years. *"For when for the time ye ought to be teachers, ye have need that one teach you again which be the first principles of the oracles of God: and are become such as have need of milk, and not of strong meat" (Hebrews 5:12).*

You shouldn't stay a babe in the Lord. You ought to grow in the Lord. Sadly, for some Christians it's difficult. They get saved and are excited about the Lord and a pastor capitalizes on their enthusiasm. He gets them overly active in the work of the church, and then preaches that if they are not there for every activity then they are not right with God. There is an activity at the church nearly every day of the week. These new Christians end up getting worn out, discouraged, and eventually break under the load that has been put on them.

It's a load that should never have been put on them in the first place (If you are new in the Lord and are being overworked for the Lord, I just want you to know that it is all right to say, "no"). Many an Independent Baptist preacher has been so concerned with growth, and is frustrated because his work is not growing like so and so's, that he has driven new converts into the ground.

They were never ready for the yoke that was put on them. Many a frustrated preacher thinks that growth is evidence of God's hand on the work, but the Bible says, *"...supposing that gain is godliness: from such withdraw thyself"* (1 Tim. 6:5b).

So what happens to these Christians? They may stay in church or they may quit. Often times they quit. Does that mean that their eternal position changes, in other words, their standing? No! Their standing is fixed. They may end up bitter and mad at God, or just disillusioned by the whole thing, but if they're saved then their standing remains the same.

I've come across Christians who are not going to church. After talking to them, I found out they used to go to a certain Independent Baptist church and all they heard were salvation messages. Every sermon was a salvation sermon. Praise God for salvation sermons, but there comes a time when the diet needs to be balanced. And so they end up leaving. Why? Hungry!

The average Pastor that is turned out of the average Christian school knows very little Bible. I had a pastor, who had a good sized church which had been built on soul winning, instead of the word of God, come up to me and ask me if I could teach him some things about the tribulation. He never learned anything about it at school.

That's a sad testimony to that school. I don't know how much the preacher paid to go there, but it was a waste of money and time.

These same pastors often make fun and ridicule those schools and students of the word of God that do know a little Bible. They have an inferiority complex. They realize they don't know anything and are afraid that their congregation is going to find out how little that they do know. So they make fun of studying the word of God.

I believe many, not all, of the pastors who propagate the heresy of Baptist Briderism are in this category. They will make statements about the Baptist church and the local church that are scripturally impossible, but they are too ignorant of the Bible to understand why it would be impossible.

That is part of the purpose of this book. That is why I am spending so much time on basic doctrine, such as your standing and state. There is many a preacher that does not even know the difference. The longer I see the mess that true Christianity is in, the more I see that the successes we have enjoyed in the past and present are due to GOD ALONE, and nothing that we have done.

The second state that a Christian can be in is:

THE CARNAL STATE

This was also mentioned back in First Corinthians 3:1-4.

> (3) For ye are yet carnal: for whereas there is among you envying, and strife, and divisions,

are ye not carnal, and walk as men? (4) For while one saith, I am of Paul; and another, I am of Apollos; are ye not carnal?

Notice the "yet." They should have grown in the Lord, but were still in the state of being carnal. This is the state of the average Christian that has been saved for any length of time and is working for the Lord. The majority of Christian workers are right here, carnal.

The word carnal is similar to the word carnivore, a meat eater, or chili con carne, which is beans with meat. So, right off the bat, you know what you are dealing with. You are dealing with the flesh. This state is a state in which you are more concerned about the flesh than you are with the spiritual. The flesh is that part of the person that is running them. Furthermore, amongst many of the Independent Baptists, this is the prevalent state. And there are three characteristics of this state.

ENVY: Those Christians, whether they are a church member or in the ministry, who have envy in their heart, are then in a carnal state. This opens up a big can of worms so to speak. The Bible says, *"Wrath is cruel, and anger is outrageous; but who is able to stand before envy?"* (Proverbs 27:4).

Envy is an attitude where you resent the superior accomplishments, or position of another, and/or desire to attain similar accomplishments and/or position, such as Cain who was envious of Abel, hated him, and ended up murdering him.

You may ask, "Could such a thing as that go on amongst God's people?"

Here Comes The Bride

There has been a case where one preacher was envious of another preacher's accomplishments and tried to frame him so he would get kicked out of the ministry. He was called to a motel late at night under the guise that a lady needed to talk to a preacher, and it was urgent.

When he got there, there were men in the closet with cameras and the plan was that the woman would force a kiss on him while at the same time they would take a picture, and make it look like he was having an affair. Fortunately, the preacher brought his wife and foiled the plot. The other preacher was caught trying to frame him. All because of envy.

It is all too common for a preacher to envy another preacher's work and desire to have a work like so and so's. Frustrated ambition! The most common problem with the pulpit and the pew today is frustrated ambition. I made mention of it earlier, but the Bible says that, *"...supposing that gain is godliness: FROM SUCH WITHDRAW THYSELF"* (1 Tim. 6:5b). *"But godliness with contentment is great gain"* (1 Tim. 6:6).

It's amazing how preachers will use that verse with regards to material possessions, but somehow miss the application to their own ministry. No, it is not a sin to desire growth, but the growth is up to God. *"I have planted, Apollos watered; but God gave the increase."* (1 Corinthians 3:6) And should be left up to God. A farmer cannot make his crops grow. All he can to is plow, plant and water.

If another preacher has a bigger work, then rejoice with those that rejoice. Don't judge your success on whether your work is as big as someone else's. At the judgment seat of Christ, you're not judged on the size of your work, or how much you did, your work is judged by the quality of the work; *"...of what sort it is"* (1 Corinthians 3:13). If many a preacher would get that through their heads there would be less envy going around.

If Jesus Christ were judged by the standards of the Independent Baptists of today, he would have to be classified as a failure. By the time that he died all of his followers forsook him and fled. Only one returned and was there at the cross when he died. By the world's standards, which is what many of the brethren go by, Jesus Christ was a failure.

Now they would not say that, and I'm not implying that they believe that. I know they don't believe that. But in practice they go by the world's rules basically, and to them, size is success. As such, many of the preachers of our day are carnal. They are in a carnal state.

I can understand a preacher who having a church that is not quite big enough to take him on for full time, having to work a job. I did that, and it will wear you out. To desire a few more members to free you up from a secular job is not what I'm talking about. That is not envy. That is working your tail off and you don't know how much longer you can last or your family can last and you need some help so you can go full time.

I'm talking about those who have a church of 100, and are envious of another brother who graduated at the same time, yet he has a work of 300. That is not of God. That is envy, it is sin, and if you don't get control of it you may end up committing murder. As

I said before, there have been many a baby Christian spiritually killed by a pastor who was trying to build a work as big as brother "so and so". The pastor felt like he was a failure if he didn't have one growing like someone else's, and he runs a babe in Christ right into the ground and throws them aside like a used rag when they are done with it. I AM NOT EXAGGERATING. I'VE SEEN IT HAPPEN!

I know of one good-hearted young Christian, who was a single man, and he ended up in the hospital from the stress that his pastor was putting on him. The power that was being wielded over him bordered on cultic.

STRIFE is another characteristic of the carnal state that a Christian can be in. Striving with one another. How many times have you tried to witness to someone about the Lord and have them bring up the issue of fighting in the church? They say to you, "All those Christians ever do is fight."

I heard a story that Evangelist Jim White told of how he had a meeting in a church and it wasn't going very well. The people wouldn't respond to anything he said. He said he tried to make them glad, but they wouldn't be glad. He tried to make them sad, but they wouldn't be sad. He tried to make them mad, but they wouldn't get mad. Finally, a few nights into the meeting he stopped in the middle of his sermon and asked the preacher, who was sitting on the front row, "Brother, what's the problem? I've got a wife at home that I'd much rather be with, this meeting is not going anywhere. What is going on?" The preacher looked up from the notebook he was writing in and said, "It's the curtains, brother," and went back to writing in his notebook.

This church had been fighting over what color curtains to get for the church sanctuary. One group wanted one color, and the other group wanted another color, and the pastor was fed up with the fighting and went out and bought a different color without asking either side. And that church was full of strife over it.

Bro. White, in order to make his point get through to them, took his shirt off and said, "Here, put this over your window. It doesn't matter what is over the windows. There is a world that is lost and dying and going to Hell!!!" Amen and Amen!! Christians fight over the strangest things, but it shows that they are in a carnal state. Envy, strife, and division are all results of being in a carnal state.

The third state is the;

SPIRITUAL STATE

This state ought to be the goal of every believer. Keep in mind you may reach a spiritual state and then drop back to a carnal state for a while, and climb back up to the spiritual state. Your state is a condition that can change and, as such, depends on your own free will. It's up to you to determine how you are going to live for the Lord. God has told you in his word what he wants from you, but it is up to you whether or not you are going to attempt to do it.

The spiritual state is not a permanent sinless state as the Holiness claim you can attain. The spiritual state is characteristic of a Christian who is walking

Here Comes The Bride

in close fellowship with God and is what I call, "God minded." He has his eyes on Jesus Christ and is going through each day mindful of the Lord's will for his life, and whether he is doing it as the Lord would have him to.

Recently I heard a missionary from Kenya by the name of McClain. He told of how the Lord was working in his field of service. He also told of how, at times, they would be without any money. One story in particular he told how his wife had asked him if they had any money, and he said, "no". She then asked, "What about the emergency fund?" He told her that was empty also. But they didn't worry nor fear. Their faith was in the Lord and they knew that they were in the Lord's perfect will for their lives.

She wanted this money to do something special for some of the native women that they were ministering to. The money was not desired even for themselves. So they prayed and the next morning they got an Email: a church back in the states had a special offering for them and the money was on the way. The McClains had not contacted anybody about their need. They just prayed for it.

There were many other things he told, and it was a testimony of a man who looked to God for everything. He was not striving with anyone. He was about the work that God had given him to do. Whether his work was as big as somebody else's meant nothing to him. He would rejoice with those with whom God was blessing. He knew what the Lord wanted him to do and that is what he was concerned with.

He also mentioned, in the course of conversation

Your State

after the service, that he had read his Bible over 100 times. From what I gathered, he spent much time in prayer and so on. Those are marks of a spiritual Christian. He has God on his mind and is concerned with what God wants him to do, period. If it isn't as big or as glamorous as another Christian's work, it means nothing to him. For the spiritual Christian is thrilled to have the opportunity to serve the Lord and is concerned with what the Lord thinks of his service, regardless of what others may say or be doing. It is a God minded service that wants to be able to stand before the Lord at the Judgement seat of Christ and have the Lord say, "Well done, thou good and faithful servant. You did what I WANTED YOU TO DO."

Whether you are a housewife or a preacher there is only one thing that will matter when you stand before the Lord. Did you fulfill his will for your life? To the spiritual Christian that is all they are concerned with. Your eyes must be on the Lord and off the brethren, your treasures in Heaven. You are running your race in your lane and running so that you may obtain.

"Know ye not that they which run in a race run all, but one receiveth the prize? So run, that ye may obtain," (I Corinthians 9:24).

What does God want you to do? Are you doing it? Bob Jones, Sr. once said, "The successful man is the man that finds out what God wants him to do, and does it." And size has nothing to do with it!!!

Whether you are a babe in Christ, or carnal, or spiritual there is one thing for sure. It will not affect your standing in any way. It will affect you at the Judgement seat of Christ, and whether or not you will reign with Christ for a thousand years. But whether or not you are saved, in the bride, married to Jesus Christ, and etc., those things are fixed in your standing in Christ.

Clarence Larkin has a good illustration in regards to your state. He says,

> "There is a vast difference between a, "SINNER'S SINS" and a "BELIEVER'S SINS." Not that God does not hate both alike, the Believer it may be the most because he sins with greater light, but the difference is not in the sin, but in the WAY GOD TREATS IT. Here is a father who sends his son and his hired servant to do a piece of work. They are lazy and inefficient, and do not do the work. He bears with them, and tries them again, but it is no use. His son and his servant are good for nothing, his son perhaps the worse of the two. Now what does he do? He discharges the servant. He puts him out of the house. He will have nothing more to do with him. But does he discharge his son? Does he send him away from the house? Does he disinherit him? Nothing of the kind. He may rebuke him, cut off his allowance, punish him worse that he punished the servant, but he will not send him away because he is his son. We see then that "Sonship" is a REAL THING. Is "Sonship" then a shield from the punishment of sin?

Does my "Sonship" make it safer for me to sin? Oh, no! It simply gives me the blessed privilege of having an Advocate, and since it is inevitable that I will sin, it is better to sin as a SON than as an unbeliever."

Rev. Clarence Larkin, *Dispensational Truth*, (Glenside, Pennsylvania) 52.

Here Comes The Bride

CHAPTER 4

THE DIFFERENCE BETWEEN THE PHYSICAL AND SPIRITUAL

This will be one of the most important chapters in this book. For when the Briders get into the Bible they will not make a distinction between the physical and the spiritual. As a matter of fact, when it comes to the word "church" in the Bible, they will say that it is always a reference to a local assembly of believers, and therefore it is always PHYSICAL. This is not true!

They have not made a distinction between the two and as *such they have not rightly divided the word of God. "Study to shew thyself approved unto God, a workman that needeth not to be ashamed, rightly dividing the word of truth"* (2 Timothy 2:15).

Before we go any further I need to define what I mean when I say "physical." When I use the word

Here Comes The Bride

physical I am referring to something that is subject to the laws of thermodynamics. In other words when something is physical it is made up of atoms and molecules and, is in this material universe and subject to the laws of the universe.

When I refer to something as being spiritual I am referring to something which is not subject to the laws of thermodynamics and is not made up of atoms and molecules. I know these are scientific terms and the Bible says to beware of oppositions of science falsely so called. So if you want a different distinction made between the two, then let's say that something that is physical is subject to time and that which is spiritual will go on out into eternity.

For example, the Local church will not be in eternity because the local church is physical. There will be no local churches in New Jerusalem. There will be no local churches in Heaven.

Some of you Briders, right now, are trying to figure out how that can't be true. You think that the local church is spiritual, don't you! But it isn't. It is physical! It is composed of physical buildings, which house PHYSICAL PEOPLE. Do you know how you can tell? It is made up of physical matter that is subject to the NATURAL LAWS of the creation.

The saints that have gone on before us are NO LONGER PHYSICAL. They have spiritual bodies that are not subject to the natural laws of the universe. (I know that the saints do not get their spiritual glorified body until the rapture (1 Thess. 4), but for the sake of discussion let me proceed as if they have already received them.) Can they be felt? Yes! Seen? Yes! Touched? Yes! Then they must be physical.

Nope! They are spiritual bodies.

Spiritual bodies will not grow old, and they will not sin or decay. They are not subject to the laws of the natural creation.

> 1 Corinthians 15:37a, "And that which thou sowest, thou sowest not that body that shall be,..." (vs. 44) "It is sown a natural body; it is raised a spiritual body. There is a natural body, and there is a spiritual body." (vs. 53) "For this corruptible must put on incorruption, and this mortal must put on immortality."

The distinction between the physical and the spiritual is essential in understanding where the Briders go wrong and end up in full blown heresy. They don't make a distinction between the two. The distinction must be made between the two, and here are some examples.

A Christian that has not gone home to be with the Lord is still in their corrupt body of flesh. Are they physical or are they spiritual? They are BOTH.

Ephesians 4:22a and 24a, *"That ye put off concerning the former conversation the old man...* (24a) *And that ye put on the new man."* Do you see the two natures? There is an old man and there is a new man. One is PHYSICAL and the other is SPIRITUAL. So, a Christian is BOTH PHYSICAL AND SPIRITUAL. Parts of the Bible refer to the physical, and parts of the Bible refer to the spiritual. IF YOU DON'T MAKE A DISTINCTION BETWEEN THE TWO YOU WILL GET MESSED UP DOCTRINALLY!

Here Comes The Bride

Here's another example. I have sitting on my desk the word of God, A.V. 1611. Is it physical or is it spiritual? Well, the book that I'm looking at is physical. How do I know that? One of these days it is going to fall apart and decay. If it doesn't fall apart and decay it is going to burn up when the universe burns up at the end of the Millennium (Rev.20, 2Pet.3).

At the same time I am well aware that it has spiritual attributes. It is holy, eternal, and forever settled in Heaven. So even though THIS COPY will not last forever, I'm aware that the word of God will last forever and I have a copy of those words.

One more example: Jesus Christ had two parts to him while he was in the flesh. He had the human side, physical, and he had the spiritual side. He was *"God manifest in the flesh"* (1 Timothy 3:16).

So when you get into a discussion on whether or not Jesus Christ could have sinned you can have two answers and both of them will be right. Can God sin? NO! Was Jesus God? Yes! Then Jesus could not have sinned. True!? Was Jesus a man? Yes! Did he have a free will? Yes! Could he as a man have sinned? YES! I can hear it now, "Heresy, Heresy...." You mean you believe that Satan tempted him knowing that there wasn't a chance that he could fall? If so then Jesus was not fully human, and could not fully take the place of the sinner. The point to all of this is THAT HE DIDN'T SIN!

One time there was a new railroad trestle that was going to be dedicated. The day came for the dedication and people came from the towns around to see it and take part in the celebration. The people from the railroad got two of their biggest engines and had them come and park on the trestle. One of the towns' people asked, "What are they trying to do, break it?" A spokesman from the railroad replied, "Those two engines will never break that trestle. We're just proving it."

As a man Jesus was tempted to sin. As God he never could sin. The point is that he didn't. You see he had two sides to him, the human and the divine. Does God get tired? No! Did Jesus get tired? Yes! Now that He is risen He is no longer subject to the laws of his creation. His physical part was gone at the resurrection.

So there is a difference between the spiritual and the physical and there are things on this earth that consist of both. These examples are you, if you are saved, your Bible, and one that I have not covered yet, THE CHURCH.

You see there is a physical church, whoops! Wait a minute, I just made the same mistake that the Briders constantly make. I said that there was "A" physical church. That is not true. THERE ARE MANY PHYSICAL CHURCHES, EVEN IF YOU LIMIT IT TO BAPTIST!

Local churches are physical churches. There are physical churches and then there is the SPIRITUAL CHURCH. Oh, the Briders hate that term, spiritual church. They try to make it fit the local church, but scripturally it is impossible. You must make a distinction between the two in order to be scriptural. C.I. Scoffield, whom the Briders criticize as often as they can, has a good statement on the church in his study Bible, pg. 1304 footnote, in reference to

Hebrews 12:23:

> "Church (true), Summary: The true church, composed of the whole number of regenerate persons from Pentecost to the first resurrection (1 Cor. 15:52), united together and to Christ by the baptism with the Holy Spirit (1 Cor. 12:12,13), is the body of Christ of which He is the Head (Eph. 1:22,23)."
> C. I. Scofield, *Scofield Study Bible* (Oxford University Press) 1304 footnote

The spiritual church is also called the body of Christ. *"Now ye are the body of Christ, and members in particular"* (1 Corinthians 12:27). When quoting this verse, a Brider will immediately say that 1 Corinthians was written to the local church.

> " Keep in mind that Paul wrote this church epistle to a literal, local, New Testament church."
> Dr. Les Potter, *The Mystical Invisible Universal "Church"*, (Calvary Publishing, Lansing MI)29

The local church, local church, local church! But they must have never read the beginning of the book, for it is not addressed solely to the local church.

Notice (I am repeating what I said in chapter 2) 1Corinthians 1:2, *"Unto the church of God which is at Corinth, TO THEM THAT ARE SANCTIFIED IN CHRIST JESUS,* (That's everybody who is saved. Oh, you say they're the saints at Corinth. They are the ones who he is referring to about being sanctified in Christ Jesus. OK, lets read on.) *called to be saints, WITH ALL THAT IN*

The Difference Between the Physical and Spiritual

EVERY PLACE CALL UPON THE NAME OF JESUS CHRIST OUR LORD, BOTH THEIRS AND OURS:"

So you see that 1 Corinthians is NOT LIMITED TO THE LOCAL CHURCH CONTEXT, BUT IS WRITTEN TO ALL OF THE SAINTS. My, my, what a little Bible reading will do to clear up private interpretation!

So the body of Christ is not limited to a local church. If it was, then you would have bodies. There would be a body of Christ in Ephesus, Galatia, Corinth and so on. There would be bodies of Christ, and a head that has MANY BODIES IS A MONSTROSITY. We all know that there is only one head, Jesus Christ, and He only has ONE BODY. "Body of Christ" is NEVER in the plural in your Bible. *"There is one body"* (Ephesians 4:4).

"And he is the head of the body, the church:" Colossians 1:18a, *"And hath put all things under his feet, and gave him to be the head over all things to the church, which is his body, the fullness of him that filleth all in all"* (Ephesians 1:22-23).

It is plain in the scriptures that the church is the body of Christ. It is not "A" local church, or "ALL" of the local churches. A Brider will use the definite article and say, "The Local Church is the body of Christ." When he does that the logical question would be:

"Which one?"

"Oh, the local Baptist church."

"Which one?"

"Independent, Fundamental, Bible Believing, Soul winning, etc. of course."

"Oh, of course. WHICH ONE?" Which Independent, Bible believing, Soul winning, Etc. Baptist Church is

THE body of Christ?

Have you ever thought about this? If God works only through the local church, and most of the material in the New Testament is written to the local church, and by the local church we mean the local INDEPENDENT, FUNDAMENTAL, BIBLE BELIEVING, ETC. BAPTIST CHURCH, how much of the New Testament would even apply to a Christian who was not a member of one of those churches? There wouldn't be much, brother, there wouldn't be much. But that is not the case.

I have in front of me a book written by Dr. Jack Hyles. It is entitled, "The Church." It is filled with the standard Baptist Bride teaching except he believes that when all of the Christians are called out in the rapture, then all Christians will become the Church. This is political fence straddling that we will get into later.

In regards to not making a distinction between the physical and the spiritual, Dr. Hyles unifies them throughout. For all practical purposes he is a Baptist Brider in practice. By saying that all will be in the bride after the rapture he can say that he is not a Brider. While at the same time he can teach and preach like a Brider, which he does. It's a political position.

On page 72 he quotes Ephesians 5:25 *"Husbands, love your wives, even as Christ also loved the church, and gave himself for it."*

He then refers to the church there mentioned as the local church.

"If anything refutes the invisible church, this

is it. [Then this is going to be important. This is the argument that will blow the universalists out of the water.] Jesus compares Himself and His church to a man and wife. Consequently, if there (is) an invisible church, then a man has an invisible wife."

   Dr. Jack Hyles, *The Church* (Hammond, Indiana: Hyles - Anderson Publishers) 72

This is what happens to a man when he starts to privately interpret the word of God. There are a number of things wrong with this line of reasoning. Dr. Hyles has used the term, "invisible," where I have used the term "spiritual", which would be the scriptural designation. The church is not invisible to Him, for he sees it all. It is invisible to the human eye.

If we could see the church then it would not be eternal. *"While we look not at the things which are seen, but at the things which are not seen: for the things which are seen ARE TEMPORAL;* [emphasis added] *but the things which are not seen are eternal"* (2 Corinthians 4:18). This is another example of the mess that a Brider gets into. Christ and the church are spiritual, a husband and his wife are physical. See what happens when you don't make a distinction between the two? Our Husband, Jesus Christ is invisible to us right now isn't he? *"The just shall live by faith"* (Gal. 3:11). I'll continue the quote from Dr. Hyles.

> "Jesus does not love an invisible church. He could have chosen another relationship to compare with. He could have chosen angels because they are invisible to us. He could have

used spirits or souls, but He chose to use the visibility of a man and his wife."

Just as I can see my wife, Jesus can also see His. If He can't He is not God. Do you see how stupid Briders can get at times? Let's go on:

> "Jesus is talking about a visible organization which is His church and His body."

The body of Christ is not an organization; it is an organism. If He is talking about "a" visible organization, then which one? There are MANY LOCAL CHURCHES. THERE IS ONLY ONE BODY OF CHRIST IN THE SCRIPTURES. You NEVER read about BODIES OF CHRIST, you only read about the body of Christ. The fact that the body of Christ is always singular is also a fulfillment of the Lord's prayer in John 17. By the way, in John 17 Jesus is not referring to a local church. Also the Gospel of John was not written to a local church, so they can't use those as explanations.

The Lord prayed, *"Neither pray I for these alone, but for them also which shall believe on me through their word; That they all may be **one**; as thou, Father, art in me, and I in thee, that they also may be **one** in us:..."* (John 17:20-21a). There is only one body of Christ. A Brider will switch the singular and plural back and forth whenever it suits his false doctrine.

You will find "CHURCHES" in the Bible. Galatians 1:2 *"...the churches of Galatia,"* Acts 9:31, 15:41, 16:5, Rom. 16:16, and many other places there are references to churches; but you NEVER FIND THE

The Difference Between the Physical and Spiritual

BODY OF CHRIST IN THE PLURAL. Why? Because those churches were physical churches and the body of Christ is a spiritual designation. There are times when the word "church" is used for this spiritual designation such as Ephesians 5:23-33: *"As Christ also loved the church, and gave himself for it;"* (vs 25).

It did not say that Christ loved the CHURCHES AND GAVE HIMSELF FOR THEM. But that is what a Brider believes. Again Dr. Hyles says in his book, *The Church*, page 156:

> "Jesus purchased, not only our salvation, but He also purchased THE LOCAL CHURCH (emphasis added) when he died on the cross."

He uses Acts 20:28 for his reference. Now do you see how nuts people get when they don't rightly divide the word of God? Why didn't he say that Christ died for the LOCAL CHURCHES, plural? Because that would obviously be heresy, so he uses the singular and hopes nobody will see the difference. Acts 20:17 *"elders of the church"*, that is the local church. Acts 20:28 *"feed the church of God"* is not the local church.

His shallow reasoning for making church of God the local church is:

> "These preachers at Ephesus could not possibly feed all believers. They could feed only that local assembly; yet, he commands them to feed the whole assembly of God which he hath purchased with his own blood."

The Bible doesn't say that. Dr. Hyles is changing

the scriptures on you. It doesn't say, "whole assembly of God", it says, *"feed the church of God."* If the church of God is singular, and it is, then when you feed a part of it you are ministering to the whole body. See 1 Corinthians 12:12-31.

> 20 "But now are they many members, yet but ONE BODY. (emphasis added) 26 And whether one member suffer, all the members suffer with it; or one member be honored, all the members rejoice with it. 27 Now ye are the body of Christ, and members in particular."

The body is one, so if you feed a portion you are feeding the whole body because it is one organism. It is a body. It is THE body of Christ, the church. If I cut my hand I have injured my hand yes, but I have also injured my body, because my hand is one with my body.

The elders of the local church at Ephesus come and are commanded to SPIRITUALLY FEED SPIRITUAL PEOPLE, (ROM.8) SPIRITUAL FOOD, AND AS SUCH WILL BE MINISTERING TO THE SPIRITUAL CHURCH, which is his body. Did you notice, "the" local church? You can use the definite article because there is a singular church that you are referring to. You must make a distinction between the physical and the spiritual or you will end up in a mess by teaching false doctrine.

When Dr. Hyles says that "Jesus purchased...the local church" he has a big problem. To be purchased is to be redeemed, and to be redeemed by the blood of Jesus Christ means you are saved. What about the members of a, (not, "the") local church THAT ARE LOST? There is illustration after illustration of church members who realized that they were lost and got saved AFTER THEY HAD BEEN A MEMBER OF THE LOCAL CHURCH. According to Dr. Hyles, they would have already been bought by the blood of Jesus Christ. Which brings me to another point.

The local church, which is physical, is composed of saved AND LOST PEOPLE. However the church, the body of Christ is COMPOSED OF ONLY SAVED PEOPLE (1 Cor. 12:13). The body of Christ has a 100% regenerated membership. The local church DOES NOT.

> 2 Cor. 13:5: "Examine yourselves, whether ye be in the faith; prove your own selves. Know ye not your own selves, how that Jesus Christ is in you, EXCEPT YE BE REPROBATES?" (Emphasis added)

Paul writes to the Corinthians and tells them to check theirselves to see if they are in the faith. Didn't they know that Jesus Christ was in them, unless they were lost? Paul is addressing those in the church at Corinth that were lost, and if there weren't any, which I doubt, it still shows THAT IT IS POSSIBLE TO HAVE LOST PEOPLE IN THE LOCAL CHURCH! Galatians 2:4 speaks of false brethren. 2 Cor. 11:13 speaks of false apostles that are transformed into ministers of righteousness.

The Chick comic book Alberto, tells of Catholic plants in the local churches who look like Christians, but are there to mess the work up. (Alberto Rivera, *Alberto Chino, California, Chick Publications*)

This is possible because the local churches are physical and are made up of physical people, who physically join the church.

That is impossible, on the other hand, to happen in the church, the body of Christ. Why? Because it is a spiritual church that is entered when the Holy Spirit immerses a new saint into it at the point of salvation. No one joins the church, which is his body, the body of Christ, that is not saved.

When the Holy Spirit baptizes you into the body of Christ that is when you get IN CHRIST. 1 Cor. 15:22 *"For As in Adam all die, even so in Christ shall all be made alive."* If you are not in Christ you are on your way to Hell. If you are in Christ then you are IN HIS BODY. There is no lost person in the church, the body of Christ.

This is why I spent so much time on the difference between your standing and state. Your standing is your spiritual position in Christ. Your state has to do with your physical service and fellowship with Jesus Christ on this physical earth.

JUDAS WAS SAVED?

By not making a distinction between the spiritual and the physical, the Briders get into a real mess. They have to believe that all of the members of a local church are saved.

"HOUSE OF GOD: 'ECCLESIA,' 'ASSEMBLY,' 'CONGREGATION.' Only baptized **believers** (emphasis added) are in it. This membership does not save, but it does add reward."

> Frank A. Godsoe, D.D.,Th.D., *The House of God A Blood-Bought Body*, (Del City, Oklahoma, 1973) 126

So, according to him, and most other Briders, only saved people are in the church. Now lets see where they start the Baptist Bride Church. Make no mistake about this. To a Brider it is very important to prove that the church started before Pentecost. They must trace it back far enough to be associated with John the Baptist. Hence we read from Buell H. Kazee in his book, *The Church and the Ordinances*, on page 40:

> "The church was founded the day the Lord called the twelve apostles and set them apart to be witnesses of His death and resurrection. This was about two years after He began His ministry."
>
> Buell H. Kazee, *The Church and the Ordinances*, (Little Rock, Arkansas: The Challenge Press, 1972) 40

So you now have the church with only saved people in it, and it started with the apostles. So the logical conclusion is that Judas was saved. Even though in John 6:70 it reads, *"Jesus answered them, Have not I chosen you twelve, and one of you is a devil? 71 He spake of Judas Iscariot the son of Simon: for he it was that should betray him, being ONE OF THE TWELVE."* (emphasis added)

Do Briders, or some Briders believe that Judas was saved?

In his book, *The House of God, A Blood Bought Body*, by Dr. Frank A. Godsoe we read: (and by the way, just after the table of contents there is a note which says that, "This book is a textbook for Arlington Baptist College and other schools use it either as a text book or reference book.") pg. 109,

> "HOW DO WE KNOW THAT THERE WAS A HOUSE OF GOD (Baptist bride church) BEFORE PENTECOST?" (He gives 9 reasons, and the 9th reason is this,) "Because Judas was an apostle, a bishop, in the house of God when he died, and his successor was elected before Pentecost."
> Dr. Frank A. Godsoe, *The House of God*, (Oklahoma, 1973) 109

Then according to Dr. Godsoe, whose book is a text book at Arlington, Judas was saved. According to him, Judas (a Devil, who is also called the Son of Perdition,) was saved by the grace of God, and washed in the blood of Jesus Christ. THAT IS SICK! THAT IS BLASPHEMOUS! THAT IS COMPLETE HERESY! WHAT A TEXT BOOK!

Briders will not make the distinction between the spiritual and the physical. Here is another example. Dr. Hyles, page 157:

> "The Bible gives no evidence that all Christians are a church. The word "church" is the ekklesia, meaning called out assembly. When did all believers ever assemble?"

The Difference Between the Physical and Spiritual

Dr. Hyles has on page 4 said that "ekklesia" meant called out group. But here he says "assembly" to tie it in with assembling at a building. At the top of page 157 he goes over the word "sanctify", and says that it means to SET APART, which is true. In his Brider mentality he is thinking physically.

In the Bible, (1 Cor. 6:11) it says, *"but ye... are sanctified... in the name of the Lord Jesus, and by the Spirit of our God."* Then every saved person is set apart from this world as a group. What's more is that every saved person has been called out of this world, literally set apart, and is seated in Heavenly places in Christ Jesus. *"And hath raised us up together, and made us sit together in heavenly places in Christ Jesus"* (Ephesians 2:6). The church, the body of Christ, is a called out group, and is assembled in Heavenly places right now.

The problem with the Briders is that they are carnally minded and can only think of physical things and have little or no insight into the spiritual realm when it comes to the church and the Christian. They are not far from the Sadducees (Acts 23:8).

Dr. Hyles, Page 158:

> "Likewise, God's people will not be a church until we are out of this heathen land and are caught up to assemble in the sky. [I'm already assembled in Heaven.] Then we become the church... [Scripture please. No scripture is given!] We are already members of the family of God. [Not me. I am a member of "HIS BODY, OF HIS FLESH, AND OF HIS BONES;" Ephesians 5:30. And so is everyone else that is

> saved.] We are going to Heaven when we die, [I'm spiritually already there.] and we are going to form a group at the rapture that will be His bride. Until then, THE CHURCH, AND THE BODY ARE THE SAME because the church is the called-out assembly and that called-out assembly is the body of Christ."

This is the kind of circular reasoning that heresies are made of. This is also the problem you get into when you go to the Greek to help form your doctrine instead of sticking to the English. Notice, until then the church and the body are the same. He is referring to the local church. WHICH LOCAL CHURCH? YOURS, I SUPPOSE?

Dr. Hyles continues.

> "Maybe this worries you a little. All of your life you have been taught that we are the bride of Christ. What I have explained in this chapter is exactly what Baptists were taught HISTORICALLY."

Here is another quote which appeals to Baptist history, known as "tradition" in other religious groups.

> "Our position is simply the historic Baptist position. We have held this position since the days of Christ's earthly ministry."
> Dr. Les Potter, *The Mystical Invisible Universal "Church"*, (Calvary Publishing, Lansing MI) 77

Forget about whether or not it is scriptural. What

matters now is that we believe historically the truths that have been passed down throughout the ages. Well then, if that is what Baptists have believed historically, (he gives no evidence for his statement) then historically the Baptists have been unscriptural.

Nuts to history! What saith the scriptures? History has been recorded by sinners, and sinners have been known to exaggerate and get things wrong from time to time haven't they? And so what if they did believe that? If it's heresy, then it's heresy! When historical beliefs become equal, or even "authoritative" along with scripture then you are on your way to APOSTASY.

EXAMPLE OF TYPICAL BRIDER TEACHING

> Pg 34
> This verse goes on to say "...and he is the saviour of the body. Here "the body" is used, of which Christ is "the head". What a beautiful metaphor! A church should operate as a unit of members, sharing pains and joys just like a physical body; and Christ is the head.
> Eph. 5:24 Therefore as the church is subject unto Christ..." It is hard for us to conceptualize a particular church itself having a relationship with Christ."
> "If Christ is not the actual head of your local church, you should find another!"
> Dr. Les Potter, *The Mystical Invisible Universal "Church"*, (Calvary Publishing, Lansing MI) 34

Eph. 5:24 states that **"the church is subject unto Christ,"** and that this subjection is an example for a wife to follow.

Well then, if this is a reference to **the** proper local church, (it isn't, but for argument sake we shall go with it) or to **a** proper local church then, according to Les Potter, Jesus Christ is the head of that local church.

So I have a question. Would the Lord Jesus Christ ever lead, or desire to have "His church" go apostate? Would the Lord Jesus Christ, the head of the "proper" local church, ever desire, or lead His church into false doctrine? The answer is no, He would not!

Les Potter believes, and is teaching here that the local church (obviously in his mind it is a proper scriptural local church. Pg 77 "Our position is simply the historic Baptist position." So it must be a Baptist or Baptistic church) is what Jesus Christ died for, and that Jesus Christ is the head of it.

> Pg 35 "...Our conception of how Christ gave Himself for a local New Testament church is often nullified as a result of the popular universal church doctrine.
>
> "<u>Let the reader not miss the importance of this.</u> The local church is meant to perceive its relationship with its espoused head."
> Dr. Les Potter, *The Mystical Invisible Universal "Church"*, (Calvary Publishing, Lansing MI) 35

Espoused means you are going to be married to Him. Ah, there is the Brider, right there! But let me get back to my thought.

If Christ is the head of the "proper" local church, and since *"the church is subject onto Christ,"* then where are all of the churches from the time of Jesus Christ up to the present?

Where are all of the PROPER local churches from five-hundred years ago? Where are all of the churches from one thousand years ago? Guess what! They went apostate and died! But the scripture states that the **church** is subject unto Christ. *Houston, we have a problem!* The church, which is His body, is subject to Jesus Christ and I'll illustrate it for you.

Local churches go apostate. That is a fact of church history. The church, which is His body and is **"subject unto Christ,"** at the rapture is going whether it wants to or not.

You get a crown for loving His appearing (2 Tim. 4:8). That shows many of the saints, including those members of a proper local Baptist church, are not going to be ready when Jesus comes. But if they have been born again, then they are going up in the Rapture **whether they want to or not**. The saints are, and thus THE CHURCH IS, subject to Jesus Christ! The local churches are not subject to Jesus Christ, well, at least they are not after One hundred years or so.

Today, being that this is the end of the church age, the subjection to Jesus Christ by a local church lasts maybe twenty five years.

The church, which is subject unto Christ is a spiritual church/body, and the local church is a physical body.

Here is another prime example of how a Brider confuses the spiritual and the physical. This is quoted from "The Bride" by James Love, Pastor,

Here Comes The Bride
Central Baptist Church, Cincinnati, OH.

> This is a great mystery, but I speak concerning Christ and the church.' "It is clear from the context of our text that the Bride is Christ's church. "There are many different churches out there, but God is not a polygamist, as the Universal Church theory promotes. There is only one bride and I believe the true Baptist church is it."
>
> James R. Love, *"The Bride"*, The Flaming Torch (Rio Rancho, New Mexico) Vol. 36, Number 6, October/November/December, 1995, 1, 10-11

This is typical of how a Brider gets messed up. He has a "local" fixation. In that I mean that whenever he sees the word "church" in the Bible, he thinks "local." It's the same way whenever a Church of Christ reads the word "baptism" in the Bible, he thinks "water."

Notice he says, "the Bride is Christ's church." He is thinking "local" church, which is obvious by what follows. However in the context of the passage in this chapter, something that is spiritual is something that is not subject to the laws of this creation and will abide forever. Jesus Christ is SPIRITUAL, AND HIS BRIDE IS SPIRITUAL. So in regards to Christ and the church as his bride, it is a spiritual reference. Did you see what he did in the next paragraph? "There are many different churches out there, but God is not a polygamist." He took the bride and made it PHYSICAL. He then implied that if you weren't a Brider then you indirectly taught that God was a polygamist, because there are many churches, i.e..

Methodist, Lutheran, Church of God etc..

Along these lines, aren't there many INDEPENDENT Baptist churches? If each one is the Body of Christ, which is what they teach, then you still have God as a polygamist. The way they get around this is to say that the "one body" is not a "numerical" singleness, but a "typical singleness."

> Dr. Thomas Cassidy, The Bible, the Baptists, and 150 Bibliography the Bride of Christ, (First Baptist Press, Spring Valley, California,)

Buel H. Kazee writes in a footnote in reference to Ephesians 4:4-6,

> "The "one body" idea is well within our grasp here...one kind of faith...One baptism must mean one kind of baptism...In the same way, could it not mean that there is only one kind of body expressed in the many bodies (churches) in the world?"
>
> Buell H. Kazee, *The Church and the Ordinances*, 71

> **"One Body"** Again, this is obviously a numeric **unity** in connection with the "<u>one spirit</u>" that works in diversities of operations... This *"one body"* is used the same way in Eph. 4:4-5. It is "one" in type and unity.
>
> It could not be clearer that "body" is a teaching metaphor for the local church.
>
> Dr. Les Potter, *The Mystical Invisible Universal "Church"*, (Calvary Publishing, Lansing MI) 28-29

You had better watch out when a man or a church starts saying that this scripture "means" this. "What this verse is really teaching is..." This is just a metaphor. The Bible says what it means and means what it says. If you have to change the meaning of a word or group of words then you are changing the Bible to fit what YOU BELIEVE, NOT WHAT IT IS REALLY TEACHING IN THE PASSAGE.

The old method was to go to the Greek and is still used by many preachers to support their private interpretation. In the Briders many are Bible believers, or say they are, and so they just have to say, "this means this etc." If you take it as it says it you will do fine.

The body of Christ is never in the plural in your Bible. Neither is the bride of Christ. The only word that is in the plural in regards to this doctrine is the word "church." This is because there are many local churches, PHYSICAL, there is only one "body of Christ," "bride of Christ," "CHURCH," and it is SPIRITUAL. If you don't make a distinction between the two, as the Bible does, then you have to change the Bible to fit your private interpretation.

Ephesians 4:4-6 *"There is one body, and one Spirit, even as ye are called in one hope of your calling; 5 One Lord, one faith, one baptism, 6 One God and Father of all, who is above all, and through all, and in you all."* This whole passage is a spiritual passage, and not physical. Everything in the passage, the body, Spirit, call, Lord, faith, baptism, God and Father, is something that will abide forever and is not subject to the natural laws of this creation, which would make them temporal.

The Difference Between the Physical and Spiritual

To be in a local church is a temporary position. To be baptized into water is to be immersed temporarily into water. So when a Brider comes to this passage he has to change it to fit his heresy. He has to make it physical in the parts that deal with baptism and the body.

For example, Herb Evans, from his article in the Flaming Torch, "The Body of Christ is Together" states:

> "There is one body, and one Spirit... One Lord, one faith, one baptism (water)." [He immediately assails those who point out that the context is spiritual by retorting,] "Do you mean that "water" baptism is not spiritual?"
> Herb Evans, *"The Body of Christ is Together,"* (The Flaming Torch, Vol.36, Number 6, October/ November/December 1995) 1-3

Yes, that's exactly what I mean! It is a physical baptism into a physical element by a physical body that does nothing spiritually to the individual at all. It is not done by the Holy Spirit, but by a physical man!

Lest you should claim that I don't believe in water Baptism let me say that I do believe in water Baptism for a new Christian. It is in obedience to the Lord's command and is a testimony to the world of your faith in Jesus Christ. There are also examples of people getting assurance of salvation and other practical benefits from it, but baptism has no effect on your standing in Christ, which means that it has no spiritual effect on the believer.

And when it comes to the "BODY", in Ephesians, A BRIDER WILL HAVE TO MAKE IT A PHYSICAL BODY, THE LOCAL CHURCH. Even though the context is spiritual.

Herb Evans in the same article,

> "We are "PLANTED" in the "LIKENESS" of his death (water baptism), identifying ourselves with both the Lord and His death. This identification initiates us into a local, visible, representative church/body."

According to a Brider, the body is a local church and you enter by baptism. They had to make it physical.

So the one body of a Brider is the local church, but then you end up with many bodies because there are many local churches. The Bible says that there is only one body and not MANY BODIES, OR MANY "ONE BODIES" of Christ. It is a spiritual body that you enter at the time of salvation, being baptized into it by the Holy Spirit. I didn't have to change a word of scripture to teach that, I just took it as it said it.

The Difference Between the Physical and Spiritual

The Contrast of the Local Church and The Body of Christ

Local Church	Body of Christ
Composed of saved and lost membership 2 Corinthians 13:6	Composed of only saved, born again people. 1 Corinthians 12:13
Found in the plural, "churches" Galatians 1:2, Acts 16:5	Never found in the plural in the word of God Ephesians 4:4, 5:30
Ends Apostate Revelation 3:14-20	Eternal in Glory with no end Ephesians 5:27
Local churches are organizations Titus 1:5	The body of Christ is an organism, His body, flesh and bone Ephesians 5:30
Works needed to join. Present yourself and baptism	Joined by Grace at Salvation. Ephesians 2:8-9 1 Corinthians 12:13
Sinful 1 Corinthians 5	Without spot or blemish Ephesians 5:27, Revelation 19:7-8
Pastor is the head 1 Tim. 3:5	Jesus Christ is the Head Colossians 1:18, Ephesians 5:23
Can leave a local church, you will at death 1 Corinthians 5:5	Cannot leave the Body of Christ Ephesians 5:30, 2 Timothy 2:11-13

Here Comes The Bride

CHAPTER 5

SEVEN BAPTISMS

As I have shown, when a Brider sees the word "church" he automatically thinks "local." That is, he always thinks of a church as a local assembly of believers and is wrong where the Bible speaks of the church in the spiritual sense. Just as it is not always a reference to a physical local assembly, so too, a Brider breaks his neck spiritually when it comes to baptism.

Now we know that baptism is one of the qualifications for acceptance into the membership of a local Independent Baptist Church, and it should be. But just as the Brider elevates the local church to a spiritual position that is unscriptural, he also elevates water baptism to a position that is unscriptural. You see whenever a Brider sees the word "baptism," he thinks "water." The same way that a pastor or member of the Church of Christ does. Though I know a Brider does not believe what a Church of Christ preacher believes, yet when it comes to the word "baptism" in the word of God he thinks "water."

He must! For if, in his mind, every reference to a church in the Bible is a local church, then every reference to baptism would therefore have to be water, because they are both in the PHYSICAL REALM. However scripturally, there are physical baptisms, and there are other baptisms. As a matter of fact there are seven baptisms in all. You say, but the Bible says that there is only "one baptism." Keep reading. I'll get around to that.

So at the start of this chapter we will get into a little more of the difference between the PHYSICAL AND THE SPIRITUAL. I have put it in this chapter since the whole chapter will be on the subject of baptism.

The subject of baptism has been a controversy ever since the start of the church. Down through the ages people have argued over baptism, and which one is the right one, etc. Christians have been killed over this doctrine because they did not agree with another church's teaching about baptism. For many years we were called "Anabaptists" because we would baptize people who had not been scripturally baptized. In other words, the Baptists would not accept infant baptism. That is not the purpose of baptism. To baptize a baby does nothing for that child spiritually.

Let's say you attend a church that does believe that baptism is needed to take away original sin, or something spiritual does take place when you baptize a baby. Along comes a person and baptizes them again after they have gotten saved. They are now saying that the first baptism was no good. That has caused a lot of blood to be shed over the years by religious people who are intolerant of other religions. Bible Believers have never killed anyone who has disagreed with them. You can't find it one time in history. You can find numerous examples of Christians being killed by Rome, and baptism was a point over which many were killed.

Now you would think that if we have the name of "Baptist," that we would put a lot of emphasis on baptism. Isn't it strange that the only group that doesn't put a lot of emphasis on baptism is the Baptists? Virtually every other religion or denomination in the world says that baptism is essential for salvation or has some sort of spiritual efficacy to the individual. The Catholics believe it's necessary. The Pentecostals believe it's necessary. The Church of Christ believes it's necessary. The Mormons believe it's necessary. But the Baptists don't. Isn't that strange? You would think from our name that we would put the most importance on it of them all, but we don't. When it comes to baptism all a true Baptist believes is that baptism gets you wet. It does nothing spiritually to the individual at all.

I say "true" Baptist because as you will see, a Baptist Brider puts more emphasis on baptism than he should, and ends up with it having a spiritual effect on the Christian that is not scriptural. A Brider leaves the true Baptist position in regards to baptism and puts a spiritual significance to it.

To start with, let's go to the Bible and see what the Bible says about baptism. As the New Testament opens, we find John the Baptist baptizing people.

Matthew 3:11, *"I indeed baptize you with water unto repentance: but he that cometh after me is mightier than I, whose shoes I am not worthy to bear: he shall baptize you with the Holy Ghost, and with fire."* In this scripture John the Baptist is down in the Jordan river baptizing people. And in the verse he mentions two other baptisms: Holy Ghost and fire. So in the verse there are three baptisms mentioned.

1. John's baptism
2. Jesus baptizing with the Holy Ghost
3. Jesus baptizing with fire

If you are familiar with your Bible you will remember that in Ephesians 4:5 it reads: *"One Lord, one faith, one baptism."* So how can John mention three baptisms, when Paul says that there is only one baptism. It seems that there is a contradiction. No, there is no contradiction. There are a total of seven baptisms in the Bible, yet there is one that stands out from all of the rest. For example, he also said that there was one Lord and one God, yet 1 Corinthians 8:5b says, *"(as there be gods many, and lords many)."* So there is more than one baptism, yet there is only one true baptism that is different from the rest.

JOHN THE BAPTIST AND HIS BAPTISM

How many times have you heard someone get up in

the pulpit and say, "Was he named John the Methodist? Or was he called John the Presbyterian? No, he was called John the Baptist," and the preacher says it like he knows what he is talking about, thinking he has just made a great statement on why you ought to be a Baptist. That man hasn't got a clue as to what he is talking about.

In his booklet, *The Church*, Wayne Cox, states:

> "Thus we establish the fact that is undeniable and indisputable, that his name was John, that his title was Baptist, and that he baptized because he was a Baptist and not vice versa...I might add that the only baptism that Christ ever had was Baptist baptism, and that the only baptism that the apostles ever had was Baptist baptism...No man, therefore, could be one of the original twelve unless he had first been baptized by John the Baptist. Christ required Baptist baptism before He ordained any of the apostles."
> Wayne Cox, *The Church*, (Liberal, Kansas: Wilderness Voice Publications) 8

These Briders always want to trace their lineage back to John the Baptist and by so doing they say that it proves that Baptists are the true Biblical line of Christianity. But there are some problems with this; for example: Luke 16:16 *"The law and the prophets were until John: since that time the Kingdom of God is preached."*

John the Baptist was a prophet who prophesied UNDER THE LAW. He was not under grace in this age for he died, in Matt. 14, before the death of the testator. Hebrews 9:16-17 *"For where a testament is, there must also of necessity be the death of the testator. 17 For a testament is of force after men are dead: otherwise it is of no strength at all while the testator liveth."*

John the Baptist prophesied under Old Testament conditions, which were the law and the prophets, not under grace with the church of God. Now this is one of the reasons that these Briders make such a big mistake when it comes to trying to teach doctrines from the word of God. They fail to *"rightly divide the word of truth."* They don't believe the Bible as it says it, where it says it and to whom it says it. It's amazing how many times, as I have studied the writings of various Briders, that they will say, "this word MEANS this." Or that a certain word is not literal, but only FIGURATIVE OR SYMBOLIC.

I am reminded of the story that a preacher told of how he went to a church and preached a meeting. After the meeting a man in the church took him home and put him up for the night. When they got there the man started to discuss Bible with him, and it went till about 2:00 A.M. Exhausted, they went to bed and got up the next morning and started in again on Bible.

It was a discussion of whether or not we should go to church on Saturday. Whether Jesus is fully God, and other various doctrinal questions. When that man was confronted with a verse of scripture he would say, "Well, it really means..." and the retort would be, but that isn't what the verse SAYS. Such as, *"before Abraham was I am"* to prove the deity of Christ. The man would say, "Well he means, before Abraham was, he was." But that isn't what it said. Haven't you ever run into this when you try to deal with a Jehovah's

Seven Baptisms

Witness? You show them something from the Bible and they say, "Well that isn't what it means, my Bible says something different." You had better watch out when a man or woman tells you a word doesn't MEAN WHAT IT SAYS. (I'll get back to John the Baptist in a little bit).

For example: Dr. Thomas Cassidy, in regards to Ephesians 4:4-5 says:

> "One body," "It is obvious here that the Bible clearly teaches there is only one body. This passage does not indicate a numerical singleness, but a typical singleness. By this I mean there is only ONE TYPE [emphasis added] of true New Testament church (called the body in Col. 1:18)."

Do you see what he did? One doesn't mean one. "ONE" MEANS TYPE. This is an example of the slick way Briders change the word of God to fit their heresy.

There is only ONE BODY! You know how I know that? Because it says that. It does NOT SAY, "ONE TYPE OF BODY." IT SAYS, "ONE BODY!" This will come out more and more as we deal with the doctrine of baptism in the word of God.

A Brider doesn't believe that there is only one body. A Brider believes that there are thousands of bodies all around the world!

As we cover baptism, the Brider will have to make the one baptism of Ephesians 4, 1 Corinthians 12:13, Galatians 3:27, and Romans 6:3-4 a water baptism; which it is not. He will have to do this by saying that what a certain word MEANS IS... No, it means what it

119

says!

If you have a hardened heart of unbelief then that is your problem. The thing to do is believe what it says as it says it, for it says what it means and means what it says. Now, let's get back to John the Baptist. John baptized under Old Testament conditions and was under the law. If you want to trace your lineage back to John, help yourself; but you'll end up under the law keeping the Sabbath, not eating ham and bacon, and so forth.

Jesus said, *"Verily I say unto you, Among them that are born of women there hath not risen a greater than John the Baptist: notwithstanding he that is least in the kingdom of heaven is greater than he"* (Matt. 11:11).

Why? Because if you are saved you are not only born of a woman, but also of God. You have been born twice.

You can't scripturally trace your spiritual lineage back to John. He wasn't born again, and he wasn't in the church, body, or bride. John is preaching in John 3:29 and says, *"He that hath the bride* (church) *is the bridegroom:* (Jesus Christ) *but the friend* (John the Baptist, representative of either Old Testament, or tribulation saints, but definitely not church age saints) *of the bridegroom, which standeth and heareth him, rejoiceth greatly because of the bridegroom's voice: this my joy therefore is fulfilled."*

John plainly says that he is not in the bride, or part of the bride, but that he is a friend of the bridegroom. John lives and ministers under Old Testament conditions, because the death of the testator has not happened, and therefore it is SCRIPTURALLY IMPOSSIBLE to tie him in with the church. There was no new testament church at that time! Notice this excellent and truthful quote from the North Star Bible Institute Manuel:

> "The church as a body is IMPOSSIBLE (EMPHASIS ADDED) without the death of Christ through whom she is reconciled to God; without the resurrection of Christ by which she partakes of His resurrection life; without the ascension of Christ by which she is assured of a Head; and without the descent of the Holy Spirit by which she is formed into an organism through the baptism of the Holy Spirit."
> "Dispensational Truth", North Star Bible Institute, pg. 151 (no publisher but the Institute was at 1st Bible Baptist Church, Rochester, New York)

Therefore you cannot trace the Baptist church back to John the Baptist. He was called Baptist because of what he was doing. He was baptizing people, and he was the only one doing it at the time. He was not a Baptist in the sense that he was a born again Christian who was a member of a local church and had a pastor over him.

John was the last of the Old Testament prophets who lived under the law, who was sent by God to prepare Israel for their Messiah by baptizing people in order to manifest Christ to *Israel. "But that he should be made manifest to Israel, therefore am I come baptizing with water"* (John 1:31b). It was a Jewish baptism of repentance for the nation of Israel.

The nation was in apostasy at the time and he was on the scene to get the nation to repent so as to be ready for their Messiah, Jesus Christ. John 1:11

regarding Jesus Christ, *"He came unto his own (Jews), and his own received him not."* Yes, it is true that he baptized in water by immersion, but that is where the similarities end.

You never read where he said, *"In the name of the Father, and of the Son, and of the Holy Ghost."* That command was given in Matt. 28. However to a Baptist Brider all he can see is that John had the label of "Baptist" attributed to him, and that he was putting people under the water, therefore he must be just like us today. This is typical Brider mentality! Find one or two things similar and then claim that everything is the same.

Notice though what happens to some people who were baptized with Johns' baptism in Acts 19:3 *And he said unto them, Unto what then were ye baptized? And they said, Unto JOHN'S BAPTISM [Emphasis added]. 4 Then said Paul, John verily baptized with the baptism of repentance, saying unto the people, that they should believe on him which should come after him, that is on Christ Jesus. 5 When they heard this, they were baptized in the name of the Lord Jesus.*

Paul does not accept John's baptism. If there ever ought to be an acceptable baptism to a Brider, it would be John's. Yet Paul does not accept it. Maybe John and his disciples had poor follow-up and a couple of people got through who were not saved. That has got to be the reason Paul re-baptizes them. Oh! Here's the reason from Wayne Cox.

> "No doubt they were baptized by Apollos (Acts 18:24-19:1) who did not have church authority. Apollos never met John the Baptist... Apollos baptized without Scriptural authority."
> Wayne Cox, *The Church*, (Liberal Kansas, Wilderness Voice Publications) 11

If this crazy statement were true, then baptism would be a means of receiving the Holy Spirit. However Paul gives them a new message of salvation that JOHN DID NOT HAVE AT THE TIME, and then baptizes them in the name of the "Lord Jesus." John's baptism was NO LONGER ACCEPTABLE. WHY? Because the testator had died, and God was now turning to the Gentiles. John's ministry was a ministry to Jews. To claim that you have ties with John the Baptist, and to try to trace your heritage back to him is to wrest the scriptures to your own destruction.

THE BAPTISM OF SUFFERING AND DEATH

The next baptism that you read about in the New Testament is found in Matthew 20:20-23. Mrs. Zebedee comes to Jesus and asks for her two sons to sit one on the right hand and one on the left in the Lord's kingdom. Included in Jesus' response is the question, *"Are ye able to drink of the cup that I shall drink of, and to be baptized with the baptism that I am baptized with?"* In Luke 12:50 Jesus says, *"But I have a baptism TO BE (it was yet future) baptized with; and how am I straitened till it be accomplished!"*

Obviously he is not talking about his baptism by John that has already occurred. And this cup, he says, the two disciples (James and John) will drink of also. Matt. 20:23 *And he saith unto them, Ye shall drink indeed of my cup.*

Here Comes The Bride

In Matthew 20, Jesus is on his way to the cross, as the immediate context of verse 18 shows. *"Behold, we go up to Jerusalem; and the Son of man shall be betrayed unto the chief priests and unto the scribes, and they shall condemn him to death."* There are only a few final discourses in Matthew after chapter 20 and then he goes to the cross.

The cup that he is referring to is his PHYSICAL suffering of death on the cross. It is not a reference to his spiritual suffering and atonement, for only the Son of God could accomplish that; in becoming sin for us who knew no sin. But when he says that James and John will indeed drink of this cup, then it has to be in a physical realm.

And in the context of verse 18, then it would be physical suffering. James is martyred in Acts 12, and John, according to *Fox's Book of Martyrs*, was thrown into a vat of boiling oil, miraculously survived, and then was exiled to the Isle of Patmos (Rev. 1). John Foxe, *Foxe's Book of Martyrs*, (Michigan: Zondervan Publishing House) 5

The cup is physical suffering. There is a little booklet as a testimony to this which is entitled:

> "The trail of blood, or following the Christians Down Through the Centuries From the days of Christ to the Present Time."
> J.M. Carroll, *"The Trail of Blood,"* (Kentucky, Ashland Avenue Baptist Church, 1988) 7

Have you ever noticed that suffering is a requirement for reigning with Christ in the Millennium? Suffering is not one of those subjects that we like to think about or mention as being part of the Christian walk, but it is.

When this cup is mentioned many turn away and thank God for eternal security. But notice Romans 8:16-18, *"...And if children, then heirs; heirs of God, and joint-heirs with Christ; IF SO BE THAT WE SUFFER WITH HIM, that we may be also glorified together."* Your inheritance is conditioned on suffering. The inheritance is said to be a REWARD in Colossians 3:24, *"Knowing that of the Lord ye shall receive the reward of the inheritance: for ye serve the Lord Christ."*

So we see that not all Christians will reign with the Lord for a thousand years. 2 Tim. 2:12, *"IF WE SUFFER, WE SHALL ALSO REIGN WITH HIM: IF WE DENY HIM, HE ALSO WILL DENY US"* (Emphasis added). You will be denied the privilege of reigning with him. There are many verses on the subject of suffering. It is not a part of the Christian walk this flesh appreciates because it has to do with the mortification of the flesh. Paul said he died daily. Not only that but Paul is said to be OUR PATTERN OF ALL LONGSUFFERING.

1 Timothy 1:16b *"...that in me first Jesus Christ might shew forth all longsuffering, for a PATTERN to them which should hereafter believe on him to life everlasting."*

If you believe on Jesus Christ then you will have to be prepared to suffer. What makes God sick of this modern Laodicean Christianity is that they have all of their bases covered and will not stick their necks out for him. They are afraid to suffer. They're carnal and lukewarm and it makes God sick!

I was in a church recently and on a bulletin board there was a picture of a man who was a natural born Iranian and a Christian pastor. He would try to start churches in Iran, and when they would shut him down he would start another one underground. Eventually they caught up with him and executed him. He died a martyr for Jesus Christ; I believe 1995 was the date. What have you done for the Lord? The cup has to do with suffering, and now we get to the baptism. Baptism is always a BURIAL in the Bible, and the context here is the cross.

We know that Jesus Christ went to Hell according to Acts 2:27, Matt. 12:40, and in Jonah 2:1-6, *"...all thy billows and thy waves passed over me." "...out of the belly of Hell cried I..."* Luke 12:50, *"But I have a baptism to be baptized with; and how am I straightened till it be accomplished!"* Obviously, this is a reference to the cross. This baptism is a baptism of death.

The Bible speaks of this baptism again in Romans 6. We know that James and John received the Lord's baptism in Acts 2. (Though they had received the Holy Spirit in John 20:22, *"he breathed on them, and saith unto them, Receive ye the Holy Ghost,"* yet it is not spoken of as a baptism; and Acts 2 is the fulfillment of Matt. 3:11, *"he shall baptize you with the Holy Ghost."*) They received the Holy Spirit and, as such, were also baptized into Jesus Christ and also into his death according to Romans 6:3-4, *"Know ye not, that so many of us as were baptized into Jesus Christ (notice it did not say water) were BAPTIZED INTO HIS DEATH?"* Don't try to change it and say, "Well it means..." Believe it!

If you are saved then you have been baptized into Jesus Christ and as such have been baptized into His death. This is made plain by Romans 6:6a, *"knowing this, THAT OUR OLD MAN IS CRUCIFIED WITH HIM."* A part of you has died, the old man, and the spiritual part of you, the new man, is now in Jesus Christ. If you are in Jesus Christ then you have died WITH him. You have been baptized into his death. That is what it says. It never mentions anything about water, so believe it as it says it.

The cup and baptism of Matthew 20 is suffering and death.

THE BAPTISM OF THE SPIRIT

I have briefly covered this baptism in the 2nd chapter in regards to your standing in Christ. Now we shall go into more detail as to this baptism. It is this truth that is essential to the child of God to understand so as to keep from getting messed up in the Brider heresy.

> 1 Corinthians 12:13, "For by one Spirit are we all baptized into one body, whether we be Jews or Gentiles, whether we be bond or free; and have been all made to drink into one Spirit."

As we have seen already, every time baptism occurs it does not have to do with water. We just covered the baptism of death, and in Matt. 3:11 there is the baptism with fire. The baptism in 1 Cor. 12:13 is the baptism by the Spirit into the body of Christ. None of these baptisms have water associated with them, or a Pastor, or a local church.

I alluded briefly to this baptism when I covered the baptism of death, because the baptism by the Spirit of God into the body of Jesus Christ must take place in order to be baptized into his death. If it is a little unclear to you at this time then this baptism should clarify it for you.

The Bible says, *"For by one Spirit are we all baptized into one body..."* So believe it. I am not going to tell you, "what this verse means is...." or "what this verse is really saying...". The Bible says what it means and means what it says. The Spirit of God baptizes you into one body. If you haven't been then *you are lost. "For as in Adam all die, even so in Christ shall all be made alive,"* (1 Corinthians 15:22).

You are either IN ADAM, OR IN CHRIST. You are either lost, in Adam, or you are saved, in Christ, which takes place when you are born again. That's why I mentioned this in the chapter on your standing and state. Your standing takes place at the point of salvation and never changes. You get put IN CHRIST.

When I got baptized at the First Baptist Church in Sonora, California, I was not baptized INTO THE BODY OF CHRIST BY THE SPIRIT OF GOD, I WAS BAPTIZED INTO WATER BY HAROLD ALEXANDER, THE INTERIM PREACHER. What happened to me? I GOT WET!!! Did my STANDING IN CHRIST CHANGE? NO! My standing in Christ is obtained BY GRACE!!!

So when you get saved you are baptized (buried or immersed, though in the Bible, baptism is referred to as a burial; which we will see) into the body of Jesus Christ. This is so strong that in Ephesians 5:30 it says, *"For we are members of his BODY, OF HIS FLESH, AND OF HIS BONES."*

That body, and that flesh, and those bones are SUPERNATURAL AND WILL NOT BE EATEN BY MAGGOTS, (as will the bodies of believers who are members of local churches, if the Lord tarries). You

Seven Baptisms

become a MEMBER of his body, and Jesus Christ ONLY HAS ONE BODY, but to a Baptist Brider Jesus Christ has MANY BODIES, CALLED LOCAL CHURCHES. The Briders are nuts!

This is carried even farther in 2 Tim. 2:13, *"If we believe not, yet HE ABIDETH FAITHFU: he cannot deny himself."* It is possible for a Christian to get so backslidden, as to deny that he even knows Jesus Christ, or even believes in him.

If you had been at the fire with Simon Peter you would have never guessed he was saved, but he was. Many people have gotten saved and God allows something to happen in their lives, which makes them mad at God, (though it is intended to purify and make them more like Jesus Christ) and they end up quitting and bitter.

Do they lose their salvation? No! Are they no longer A MEMBER OF CHRIST? Of course not! They are part of him, a member of his body, and *"HE CANNOT DENY HIMSELF!"* This is explained also in 1 Corinthians 12:14-27, *"For the body is not one member, but many. (15). If the FOOT shall say..."* It's talking about being a member of THE body, not "A" body.

I was driving to work one morning and came upon a wreck. A car had collided head on with a tractor trailer. It was a horrible accident and help was already there. As I slowly drove by I noticed a man with a clean towel in his hand walk to a certain spot on the shoulder of the road and pick up an object that was lying there. It turned out to be the arm of the woman who had been driving the car. She had been dismembered in the accident.

Though it is a gruesome story, it illustrates the

point. A body has members, such as a foot, arm, eye, etc., just like it mentions in 1 Corinthians 12. Every person who is saved is IN THE BODY OF CHRIST, and has been placed there by the Spirit of God.

That's why it says in verse 27, *"Now ye are the body of Christ, AND MEMBERS IN PARTICULAR."* You are ALL IN THE BODY, but not all have the same job. You have all been placed in that body by God. 1 Corinthians 12:18 *"But now hath God set the members every one of them in the body, as it hath pleased him."*

This is a spiritual baptism that God carries out. It is an *"operation of God"* that He carries out. In Col. 2:11-12, notice in verse eleven that there is a circumcision made *"WITHOUT HANDS"* (God does it, not man) where your flesh is cut loose from your soul; it has been "put off". You are "BURIED" with him in baptism, and also raised "through the faith of the OPERATION OF GOD," NOT THE OPERATION OF YOUR PREACHER, AND NOT BY THE BAPTISM OF YOUR PREACHER! It is the operation of God that carries this out.

Did you notice in Romans 6:3-4 that if you are in Jesus Christ then you are in his death. *"Know ye not, (many Briders don't) that so many of us as were baptized into Jesus Christ were baptized into his death? 4 Therefore we are buried with him by baptism into death..."* Now in Col. 2:12 if you are in Jesus Christ then you are *"BURIED with him"* and *"RISEN with him,"* and what's more you have been *"crucified with Christ"* in Gal. 2:20.

In plainer words once you GET IN JESUS CHRIST then you are spiritually crucified, buried, and risen from the dead with Jesus Christ. And if we are risen with him then, *"as he is, so are we in this world"* (1 John

4:17). You need not wonder why it is impossible to lose your salvation. You are spiritually, already risen from the dead, in Jesus Christ and are seated in heavenly places, *"IN CHRIST JESUS"* (Ephesians 2:6).

The key to all of these truths is that in order for these things to be true you must be IN JESUS CHRIST and you are baptized into him when you get saved. Galatians 3:27 says *"For as many of you as have been baptized into Christ [NOT WATER] have put on Christ."*

When you got saved you were baptized into Jesus Christ by the Spirit of God, which was into his body, and as such you have put on Christ. He covers your soul and as such you have his righteousness, since he is your righteousness. 2 Corinthians 5:21, *"That we might be made the righteousness of God IN HIM"* (Emphasis added). But these things can only be so if you have been baptized INTO HIS BODY.

Now the Briders claim that the baptism of 1 Corinthians 12:13 is baptism by a proper Baptist preacher into water thus placing you into a local church, which, in their HERETICAL view, is the body of Christ. Notice this quote from, Herb Evans, Flaming Torch, Fall 95, page 2:

> "We are 'PLANTED' in the 'LIKENESS' of his death (water baptism), identifying ourselves with both the Lord and his death. This identification initiates us into a local, visible, representative church/body."

What local church was the Ethiopian Eunuch initiated into in Acts 8?

His comments are in regards to 1 Corinthians

12:13. He is completely wrong on this verse. Though his statement is true in regards to water baptism for a Christian, it identifies a Christian with the Lord Jesus Christ. But this passage is not talking about water baptism. I need more than just AN IDENTIFICATION WITH JESUS CHRIST. I NEED TO BE IN HIM!!! AND SO DO YOU IF YOU WANT TO GO TO HEAVEN!!! Did you notice that last part of 1 Corinthians 12:13?

It's amazing how the Briders stop with the first part of the verse but don't explain the whole verse. The rest of the verse is very important. Notice, *"whether we be Jews or Gentiles, whether we be bond or free; AND HAVE BEEN ALL MADE TO DRINK INTO ONE SPRIT"* (Emphasis added).

Do you mean to say that a person who has not been baptized into the local Baptist church has not been made to drink into one Spirit? That is the logical conclusion of the Brider Heresy. The verse says that when you are baptized into that one body then you are made to drink into that one Spirit.

So to a Brider only the saved people, who are members of scriptural Baptist churches, which, to them, is the true church with authority, can drink of the Spirit. (Notice the change to singular, I'm writing like they do for emphasis.) Now I have never read this from a Brider, but to take the whole verse you would have to come to this conclusion.

I drank of the Spirit before I ever set one foot in church. I was saved at home kneeling by my bed at 1:00 A.M. on November 29th, 1977, and that night I took the greatest drink of the Spirit of God that I ever have. I got saved that night and I have drank of that

Spirit ever since. AND ALL THAT ARE SAVED HAVE BEEN MADE, HAVE BEEN MADE, and HAVE BEEN MADE, TO DRINK INTO THAT ONE SPIRIT.

To teach otherwise is to teach a heresy and would mean that if you were not a member of a true Baptist church that you would be on your way to Hell. There would be no salvation outside of the Baptist church if you limit 1 Corinthians 12:13 to a Baptist church; for they would be the only ones who could drink of the Spirit.

In summary, the baptism by the Spirit of God is the Spirit taking a person at the time of salvation and immersing, or burying them, into the body of Jesus Christ (1 Corinthians 12:13, Gal. 3:27, Romans 6:3-4, Col. 2:11-12). Along with this immersion into the body of Jesus Christ, the Christian is also *SEALED UNTO THE DAY OF REDEMPTION* (Ephesians 4:30), by the Holy Spirit. You are not only in his body, you are in the Holy Spirit also. *"But ye are not in the flesh, but IN THE SPIRIT, (Emphasis added) if so be that the Spirit of God dwell in you"* (Romans 8:9a).

I bring this out to show that this baptism also is the fulfillment of the baptism with the Spirit in Matt. 3:11: *"...he shall baptize you with the Holy Ghost..."*

Here Comes The Bride

CHAPTER 6

SEVEN BAPTISMS

PART 2

BELIEVERS BAPTISM

Believers Baptism is the baptism referred to by the Briders when they talk about baptism. To them there is "one baptism," quoting Ephesians 4, and this is the one that they have in their minds. The difference is that the one in Ephesians 4 is spiritual and this one is physical. They do get the two mixed up, don't they? This baptism is done by a physical man placing a physical body into physical water, and is a testimony to a physical world.

Acts 8:35 "Then Philip opened his mouth, and began at the same scripture, and preached unto him Jesus. 36 And as they went on their way, they came unto a certain water: and the eunuch said, See, here is water; what doth hinder me to be baptized? 37 And Philip said, If thou believest with all thine heart, thou mayest. And he answered and said, I believe that Jesus Christ is the Son of God. 38 And he commanded the chariot to stand still: and they went down both into the water, both Philip and the eunuch; and he baptized him. 39 And when they were come up out of the water, the Spirit of the Lord caught away Philip, that the eunuch saw him no more: and he went on his way rejoicing."

Here we have a Gentile who was baptized. And there are some things to notice about it. This occurs in chapter eight. To those of you who have studied numerology in the Bible, eight is the number of a NEW BEGINNING. Eight in your Bible starts something new.

Seven is the number of completion. Seven days in a week and the eighth day starts a new week, thus becoming the first day of the next week. The eighth chapter is about Noah leaving the ark and starting a new beginning on this earth. And 2 Peter 2:5, tells us Noah is the eighth from Adam.

So why is this important? Because the eighth chapter of Acts is showing that God is starting a new thing by turning from Israel and going to the Gentiles with salvation by grace through faith. This is the first Gentile to get baptized after salvation as a testimony of his salvation. He is not getting baptised to receive the Holy Spirit as in Acts 2:38, which we will get into next.

Notice, his baptism was out of a testimony to what

he had done, which was believe on the Lord Jesus Christ. That is WHY HE WAS BAPTIZED. He was not baptized to identify himself with BELIEF. Briders will say that baptism identifies you with what you believe. This is not so! Scriptural baptism which is immersion, is a testimony to the fact that you are now a born again Christian. It is to identify you with the Lord Jesus Christ and his death, burial, and resurrection.

CHURCH MEMBERSHIP IDENTIFIES YOU WITH BELIEF, BAPTISM IDENTIFIES YOU WITH THE LORD JESUS CHRIST!!! You have got to get that straight. How can you expect a new babe in Christ to know what correct doctrine is or is not? They are a babe in Christ.

I know a lady who was saved in a Church of Christ denominational church. She was also baptized there. Are they heretical in their beliefs? Yes! Do they believe in baptismal regeneration? Yes! Is their baptism unscriptural? If it is part of the person's salvation, yes!

This lady came to my church, and she and her husband wanted to join. I knew him from way back and new that he was scripturally baptized, but I didn't know her too well. So I asked her if she had been scripturally baptized, and she said, "Yes." I'm not sure how I found out that it was in the Church of Christ, but I did.

So I asked her if she was baptized in order for her to be saved, and she said, "No." I asked her if when she was baptized was she doing it to get saved, or as part of her salvation, or did she know that she was already saved and was doing it as a testimony for the

Lord. She replied that she did it as a testimony to the world that she was now a Christian and she was doing it for the Lord. She knew that it had nothing to do with her salvation.

Out of a sincere love for the Lord she was baptized. When she was baptized she was identified with the Lord Jesus Christ, and when she and her husband joined my independent Bible Believing Baptist church she was identified with our beliefs. Baptism identifies you with the Lord. Church membership identifies you with belief.

Now if someone comes from a Methodist church and was saved there, but was sprinkled, then that is not a scriptural baptism, and they need to be scripturally baptized.

In regards to this issue though, a Brider will say that a Baptist church is the only true church and as such a Baptist preacher is the only one with AUTHORITY TO BAPTIZE. Nobody else has the AUTHORITY to baptize.

I even know of one man who left the Southern Baptist church and had to be re-baptized in order to join an independent Baptist church. If, according to the Briders, baptism identifies you with belief, then you had better get baptized every time you change your church membership. For it is extremely rare that any two Baptist churches believe EXACTLY the same on every thing.

Authority? You'd better watch out when you get to the place where you believe God has given you special authority just because you have your doctrine straight. AT LEAST YOU BELIEVE THAT YOU HAVE YOUR DOCTRINE STRAIGHT. I'm sure there are many Independent Baptists who would disagree with you on a number of different doctrines. *"Wherefore let him that thinketh he standeth take heed lest he fall."* (1 Corinthians 10:12)

It was the chief priests, the ones associated with crucifying Jesus Christ, that asked, *"By what AUTHORITY doest thou these things? and who gave thee this authority?"* (Matthew 21:23b) Won't the Judgement seat of Christ be a sight? There are going to be many surprises, to say the least!

When the eunuch was baptized he did not become a member of a church of any kind. By that I mean a local assembly of any kind. He went on his way back to Ethiopia.

If, as the Briders claim, the local church is the body of Christ, then this believer never became a member of the body of Christ. That would be the logical conclusion to their line of thinking. Obviously, it is wrong. Any statements about him starting or joining a church can only be conjecture, for the scripture gives no more information about the eunuch. As Dr. Sam Gipp puts it,

> "We notice that the eunuch, upon baptism, did not become a member of "The First Baptist Church of Jerusalem." A church that he NEVER attended. Upon confronting Acts 8:38, the "Baptist-Briders" have their bubble burst, and will have to quit pretending that Scripture teaches something which it does not. They feebly argue, "When I baptize somebody it makes them a Baptist, (scripture please) so when John the Baptist baptized Jesus, what did it make him?" The answer...WET!"
> Dr. Samuel C. Gipp, Th.D, *A Practical & Theological Study of The Book of Acts,* (Shelbyville, Tennessee: Bible and

As for the mode of baptism that was used to baptize the eunuch, it was by immersion. For the Bible says that they both came up out of the water. Obviously, they did not both go under the water, but both went down into the water and the eunuch was baptized by immersion, otherwise there would be no reason to go INTO the water. Baptism is a burial and as such scriptural baptism is immersion under the water picturing death and burial. When a person dies he is buried. He is not stood up and sprinkled with dirt on his head.

Another example of believers' baptism is found in Acts chapter ten with Cornelius. "47 *Can any man forbid water, that these should not be baptized, which have received the Holy Ghost as well as we? 48 And he commanded them to be baptized in the name of the Lord. Then prayed they him to tarry certain days.*"

Notice that they had "RECEIVED THE HOLY GHOST" BEFORE they were baptized. They were already drinking of that one Spirit.

As a testimony to their stupidity, the average Brider will try to make 1 Corinthians 12:13 water baptism. It doesn't work! There are a couple of other references to this baptism. 1 Peter 3:21 *"The like figure whereunto even baptism doth also now save us (not the putting away of the filth of the flesh, but the answer of a good conscience toward God,) by the resurrection of Jesus Christ:"*

This baptism is for a good conscience toward God. It has nothing to do with washing away sin. It is a testimony to the fact that you have believed on the

Lord Jesus Christ and by being baptized are a testimony of his resurrection; that he arose from the dead and you will too. Notice that it says, *"like figure."* It is a picture of the death, burial, and resurrection of Jesus Christ. So when someone is baptized in a sense they are preaching the Gospel as given in 1 Corinthians 15:1-4. But it doesn't stop there, for it is also a picture of the sinner being crucified, dying spiritually (Galatians 2:20), and being buried (Colossians 2:11-12). There's the baptism, baptized into Jesus Christ, and then being risen a new man in Jesus Christ (Ephesians 2:6).

Another example of this baptism is found in Acts 16, the Phillipian jailer. And the text that is used most for this baptism is Matthew 28:19-20. Spiritually there is nothing wrong with applying this baptism to the believer, though doctrinally it won't work. Did you ever notice that nobody in the Bible was ever baptized with someone saying, "In the name of the Father, and of the Son, and of the Holy Ghost?" Peter baptized them in the name of Jesus Christ, Acts 2:38. Did you notice that in Matthew 28:19 it says, *"in the NAME,"* singular? It doesn't say "names", plural, but "name." The Father, Son and Holy Ghost can all go by one name, notice. The Holy Spirit in 2 Corinthians 3:17 is called, "Lord". *"Now the Lord is that Spirit: and where the Spirit of the Lord is, there is liberty."*

Jesus Christ is called the Lord in many places, for example: *"And he said, Who art thou, Lord? And the Lord said, I am Jesus whom thou persecutest"* (Acts 9:5a). God the Father is called Lord. *"The Lord said unto my Lord, Sit thou on my right hand"* (Matthew 22:44a).

There is a name that all three personages of the

trinity go by and that is Lord. When a person is baptized in the name of the Lord, they are being baptized in the name of the Father, and of the Son, and of the Holy Ghost. This is the name that they were baptized by in Acts 10:48. Now, when I baptize I still say the usual, in the name of the Father, and of the Son, and of the Holy Ghost, but I wanted to show that Acts 10:48 could qualify for the Matthew 28 baptism.

In summary, this is a PHYSICAL BAPTISM that identifies the believer with JESUS CHRIST, NOT HIS BELIEFS. It is done after salvation, and AFTER the person has already been made to drink into one Spirit, according to 1 Corinthians 12:13, thus making it a different baptism. It's a testimony to the world of the gospel, and the believer's new life in Jesus Christ.

BAPTISM UNTO MOSES

This baptism is found in 1 Corinthians 10:1-2, and is the first baptism given to people in the word of God historically.

> "1 Moreover, brethren, I would not that ye should be ignorant, how that all our fathers were under the cloud, and all passed through the sea; 2 And were all baptized unto Moses in the cloud and in the sea;"

This happened when the children of Israel were leaving Egypt and passed through the Red Sea, and I don't mean the sea of Reeds, like the apostate

Christian schools teach.

In the back of my Bible I have various maps, and one of the maps is the route of the exodus into the wilderness. And the route given on the map is a route that takes the children of Israel AROUND the Red Sea.

My son bought me a new Bible for my birthday and in the back are maps from the Moody Bible Institute. And they have the route of the exodus going north of the Red Sea. I have maps on my computer of the exodus, PC Bible Atlas, and they have them going north of the Red Sea. That's what happens when you don't believe you have the word of God.

The majority of maps on the market today come from people, schools and companies that don't believe they have the preserved inerrant word of God, and as such don't believe what it says about Israel going THROUGH THE RED SEA.

I wonder what they do with 1 Corinthians 10:1-2? If, in their view, Israel went through marshy ground, then what are you going to do with the baptism unto Moses? They either had to teach that the Israelites were extremely short, or they have to go to "the Greek" and change it to fit their belief, thus ending up in error.

The blood of the lambs had been applied to the doors of the Israelites houses. That night the Lord came through the land of Egypt and suffered the "Destroyer" to smite the firstborn in every house that didn't have the blood of a lamb applied to the door post, from the cattle in the field to the people in the houses. Israel left Egypt that night.

Do you remember when you left Egypt by the blood

of the Lamb? After three days they came to the Red Sea and Moses stretched his rod out towards the sea and it parted. And the children of Israel passed through that sea on dry land.

The word of God says that it was a baptism unto Moses. There was a cloud over that gulf of the waters. They had water on each side and on top of them, though it did not touch them. This was a baptism by aspersion. And as such it identified them with Moses, for they were baptized unto Moses.

PETERS BAPTISM TO ISRAEL ACTS 2:38

For those of you who do not rightly divide the word of God (2 Timothy 3:15), you will have a hard time with this baptism. Acts 2:38 is the "kingpin" so to speak for those who believe in baptismal regeneration, which is the teaching that you have to be baptized in order to be saved.

I will not spend too much time with this baptism as it does not have much to do with the Baptist Briders.

In Acts chapter two we have Simon Peter preaching to Jews. It is fifty days after the Passover (Leviticus 23:15). There is no New Testament written, and all of the Jews are living as under the law. That is, if you were to put ham, shrimp, or catfish in front of them to eat, they would decline and think you were a godless pagan for suggesting such an act. The revelation of Colossians 2:14 wasn't known yet. Simon Peter is the one doing the preaching

Seven Baptisms Part 2

(Galatians 1:7-8) to the Jews who were present at this Jewish feast. All of the scriptures had been fulfilled that needed to be in order for the Lord to come back at the Second Advent to establish his kingdom on this earth for 1000 years.

John the Baptist would have fulfilled the scriptures for Elijah (Mark 9:11-13). The nation of Israel is being given the opportunity to NATIONALLY repent and turn to their Messiah, whom they had just crucified. Notice the context as we go through the scriptures.

It is a Jewish feast. The feast of Pentecost, in Acts 2:1, *And when the day of Pentecost was fully come.*

Jews had come from all over to be there. Acts 2:5 *And there were dwelling at Jerusalem Jews, devout men, out of every nation under heaven.* Also Acts 2:9-12.

Signs are being used to get the message across to the Jews. In 1 Corinthians 1:22 it states that, *The Jews REQUIRE A SIGN.* Signs started with Israel under Moses in Exodus 4. Then we read in 1 Corinthians 14:21-22 that tongues are a sign to the Jews. What's more, the tongues in Acts 2:8-11 are known languages. *Acts 2:8 And how hear we every man in our own tongue, wherein we were born? 9 Parthians, and Medes, and Elamites, and the dwellers in Mesopotamia, and in Judaea, and Cappadocia, in Pontus, and Asia, 10 Phrygia, and Pamphylia, in Egypt, and in the parts of Libya about Cyrene, and strangers of Rome, Jews and proselytes, 11 Cretes and Arabians, we do hear them speak in our tongues the wonderful works of God.*

The true signs END AS THE LORD TURNS TO THE GENTILES. 1 Timothy 5:23, 2 Timothy 4:20, Romans 1:17.

The sermon in Acts 2 is addressed to the nation of Israel, Acts 2:36, which is the reason for the question, *"what shall WE do?"* in verse 37. This is a far cry different from the question in Acts 16:30, *"What must I do to be saved?"*

EXPLANATION: Simon Peter is preaching to the Jews there present at the feast of Pentecost. The other eleven apostles are preaching in tongues, translating the message, and witnessing to the people then present.

This draws a large crowd of Jews to come and see what is going on. When Simon Peter sees the crowd he lays hold on the opportunity to preach and tells them that they as a nation have just rejected, and crucified their Lord. *"...Ye have taken, and by wicked hands have crucified and slain..."* (Acts 2:23b). *"Therefore let all the house of Israel know assuredly, that God hath made that same Jesus, WHOM YE HAVE CRUCIFIED, (Emphasis added) both Lord and Christ"* (Acts 2:36).

He makes direct application to the house of Israel, as well as those listening to him preach, that they had crucified Jesus Christ. Peter and those preaching there were all witnesses of his resurrection, proving that Jesus was the Lord. Acts 2:37 *"Now when they heard this, they were pricked in their heart, and said unto Peter and to the rest of the apostles, Men and brethren, what shall we do?"* Not, "what must I do to be saved?"

What they are saying is that in view of the fact that we have just crucified the Lord, our Messiah, what do we do now? Simon Peter tells them to, *"...Repent, and be baptized every one of you in the name of Jesus Christ for the remission of sins, and ye shall receive the gift of the*

Holy Ghost" (Acts 2:38b).

Repent of crucifying the Lord Jesus Christ, and get baptized in his name. This is not the baptism that the gentile Christian is to observe. The baptism in Acts 2 is neither for a Gentile, nor for a testimony of his salvation.

Now here are some observations about Acts 2 in regards to the Briders. I have heard on several occasions the church in Acts 2 referred to as the "First Baptist Church of Jerusalem." Sometimes this is said "tongue in cheek," but others are serious when they say it. There are some problems when you make this statement.

The church in Acts 2 speaks in tongues. These were scriptural tongues differing from the Satanic counterfeits in the charismatic churches of our day. The message was to repent and be baptized IN ORDER TO RECEIVE THE GIFT OF THE HOLY GHOST.

Baptism, a work, was plainly needed to receive the Holy Ghost. The Holy Ghost is received today by believing on the Lord Jesus Christ. No works are needed. You can repent and be baptized today and go straight to Hell. You had better go to Acts 16 and go to Heaven, rather than stay in Acts 2 and go to Hell.

Another difference is that they lived by *"the apostles' doctrine"* (Acts 2:42) and had the apostolic signs of Mark 16:17, *"And these signs shall follow them that believe; In my name shall they cast out devils; they shall speak with new tongues; 18 they shall take up serpents; and if they drink any deadly thing, it shall not hurt them; they shall lay hands on the sick, and they shall recover."* Acts 3:6; *"Then Peter said,...In the name of Jesus Christ of*

Here Comes The Bride
Nazareth rise up and walk."

Another part of this doctrine was that they *"sold their possessions and goods, and parted them to all men, as every man had need"* (Acts 2:45).

The converts in Jerusalem, who were mainly Jewish, ended up in apostasy being zealous of the law (Acts 15:4-5, 21:20).

If I was going to identify myself with anybody, I would go to Acts 11:26, not Acts 2! The church at Jerusalem does not resemble an independent Baptist church at all.

BAPTISM WITH FIRE

When we started this subject of baptism we started with Matthew 3:11, which has three baptisms in the verse itself. There is John's baptism, the baptism with the Holy Ghost, and with fire.

Only one out of these three is water, the other two are something else. *"I indeed baptize you with water unto repentance: but he that cometh after me...: he shall baptize you with the Holy Ghost, and with fire:"* (Matthew 3:11). This fire is not the cloven tongues *"like as of"* fire that are mentioned in Acts 2. To be baptized is to be immersed, and tongues as fire on your head is not a baptism of fire.

Notice in verse eight that John is preaching repentance and telling them to get right. He then likens people to trees and says, *"...Therefore every tree which bringeth not forth good fruit is hewn down and cast into the fire"* (Matthew 3:10b). [Did you know that people in the Bible are likened to trees? Mark 8:24,

Judges 9:14-15]. Then in verse 12b he says that he will, *"gather his wheat into the garner; but he will burn up the chaff with UNQUENCHABLE FIRE."* It's a reference to Hell fire.

Not only this but in Rev. 20:14, *"death and hell were cast into the lake of fire."* That is some baptism there. There is no sprinkling to it. The lost end up submerged in fire.

These last two chapters have covered the seven baptisms given in the word of God. As with the standing of the believer in Christ, the baptisms were necessary to cover, to show how the Briders get messed up by not knowing very much Bible.

There are seven baptisms, yet one true baptism. Just like there are many gods, yet one true God. There are many bibles, yet there is one true Bible. There are many churches, yet there is only one true church. If you say the local Baptist church is the one true church, then WHICH LOCAL INDEPENDENT BAPTIST CHURCH IS THE ONE TRUE CHURCH? There is only one.

Here Comes The Bride

CHAPTER 7

SIMILARITIES BETWEEN THE NICOLAITANS AND THE BAPTIST BRIDERS

Briderism gives superior power to a sinner who happens to be a pastor. The pastor has the power to kick someone out of the church, which, if what they believe is true, is in essence kicking them out of the body of Christ and changing their position in Heaven for all eternity.

So now your destiny is in someone else's hands. That's a scary thought!!! As I have shown in earlier chapters, when a person gets saved they become a member of the body of Christ. This is true of all that are saved. But the Baptist Brider believes that you must be a member of a local Independent Baptist church to be in the body of Christ; for "the" local Baptist church, to them, is "the" body of Christ.

Now think with me for a minute. If the local Baptist

church is the body of Christ, which is the bride of Jesus Christ, and the ones that make up the bride are the ones that will be the inhabitants of New Jerusalem (Rev.21); then the pastor of such a church has tremendous power. In the Independent Baptist Brider Church he has the power to kick someone out of the body of Christ and CHANGE THEIR POSITION IN ETERNITY.

If you are not in the body, you are not in the church. If you are not in the church, then you are not part of the bride. If you are not part of the bride then you will not be married to Jesus Christ, and you will not dwell in New Jerusalem. According to their doctrine a SINNER NOW HAS THE POWER TO KICK YOU OUT IF HE WANTS TO.

Dr. Thomas Cassidy states,

> "Members of the church who err IN DOCTRINE (emphasis added) or conduct shall be subject to discipline and/or dismissal..."
> Dr. Thomas Cassidy, *"A Philosophy of Baptist Ministry,"* (Spring Valley, California: First Baptist Church Publications, 1995)

(While I believe in church discipline, keep in mind the context of this discussion; your eternal destiny is now in the hands of a sinner, if what the Briders teach is true.)

"Oh, but my pastor is a good man and he would never..." Yes he probably is a good man. But I've seen some things over the years. I have seen good members of churches cross their pastor one time and he goes ballistic on them. I'm sure that this is the exception, and most pastors are good men, but it still illustrates the point. In Brider doctrine, power has been given to a man that enables him to change your eternal position in Heaven.

Now, the Brider doctrine is unbiblical and a heresy,

but how many Christians get caught up in this trap? They suffer needlessly at the hands of an insecure man in the pulpit who doesn't know much Bible, and uses fear, guilt and manipulation to run his church.

Where the Spirit of the Lord is there is LIBERTY, NOT BONDAGE AND FEAR!

This kind of setup resembles a system that God says, "HE HATES." Notice what the Bible says in Revelation 2:6 and 15. *"6 But this thou hast, that thou hatest the deeds of the Nicolaitans, which I also hate." "15 So hast thou also them that hold the doctrine of the Nicolaitans, which thing I hate."*

In Revelation 2:6, we read of the first church period after the apostles, approximately 90 A.D. - 200 A.D. The early church Christians were losing their first love, but still hated the deeds of the Nicolaitans, which God praises them for, for he hates their deeds also. But in verse fifteen the church, by then, using the seven churches as periods in the church age, had EMBRACED the doctrine of the Nicolaitans, and God rebukes them for it and states again that he hates it.

The name "Nicolaitans" is significant in that it is a combination of two Greek words; "nikao," which means to conquer, overcome, vanquish, or subdue and "laos," which means the common people. We get the word laity from this Greek word. Nicolaitan means to conquer or overcome the common people.

To make application then, this was a religious system where the clergy, or leaders of the church, or churches, would gain power over the common people who attended those churches. It was the clergy ruling over the laity. Dr. Hyles mentions this in his book "The Church" on page seventeen. However he limits the Nicolaitan doctrine to influence from outside the local church.

While I agree with this statement, I believe it goes farther than that. It can happen within a local church when the man in the pulpit OVERLY exalts his office.

A pastor is to have authority to run his church. He is to take the word of God and *"reprove, rebuke, exhort with all longsuffering and doctrine"* (2 Timothy 4:2). When you get to the point where you hear statements like, "Don't question Pastor," "Pastor is always right," and people have a fear of touching or going near the pulpit, then you are on shaky ground.

I personally have heard one famous pastor say that he tells his college students who they should and should not marry. This was within the scriptural context of saved husbands and wives, not lost or backslidden unions being considered (for then a pastor does have the right to warn against it).

Can you imagine that? The preacher was telling people who they should marry. And the ones told would have to accept it as the will of God. They would not be able to disagree, for then they would be accused of being out of the will of God. That is classical Nicolaitanism.

I greatly appreciate one pastor whom I have gone to for advice. Each time if I asked him what he thought I should do, he would say, "I can't tell you what to do, but here is what the Bible says, beyond that you are going to have to find out what God wants you to do." That is so contrary to the average Independent Baptist Church.

The average counsel is to tell you what God's will for your life is, and if you disagree with your pastor, then you are accused of being out of the will of God and backslidden. Whatever happened to the priesthood of the believer?

The temptation for people is to have them ask someone else, "tell me what to do." That's how cults are formed. No, I am not saying that the Baptist Brider churches are cults, or a cult. But I've seen people live in fear of their preacher, and have no liberty to disagree with him whatsoever. They are not even allowed to compare what he says to what the Bible says, which is Nicolaitanism in the true sense.

If what your preacher says differs from the word of God, then you had better go by the word of God. Otherwise you are headed right back to Rome.

In most of the Old German Baptist Churches, and other Amish type churches, they have kept the practice of having the preacher on the same level as that of the congregation. They preach from the floor in order to make the point that the man speaking is not any different from those who sit in the pew.

I agree with this point; though, if there is a large number of people, an elevated pulpit is better for the practical reasons of seeing the speaker and hearing him. Just make sure the reasons stay in the practical realm and don't end up with a man who is elevated above the common people.

A church where the pastor has the power to change your eternal position in Heaven is a church which has adopted an aspect of the doctrine of the Nicolaitans, which God hates.

In the article in chapter one, the excerpt from the sermon by Dr. Thomas Cassidy, *"The Bible, The Baptists,*

Here Comes The Bride
and The Bride of Christ," did you notice what he said?

> "Every pastor must be made to understand that his job is to: Pray, Prepare, Preach, Protect, Preserve, and PERFECT [emphasis added] the flock. The pastors final task will be to Present the church, [notice how he uses the word church in reference to a local church, and then calls it THE bride, so he ends up with MANY BRIDES] the Bride of Christ, FAULTLESS [emphasis added], a chaste virgin, to the Bridegroom, the Lord Jesus Christ, at the Marriage Feast of the Lamb."

In order to present it faultless, he may decide that you shouldn't be a part of his congregation, for who knows what reason and kicks you out. Five minutes later the rapture takes place and you end up in eternity as part of the family of God, but not in the bride, married to Jesus Christ.

Now that is not going to happen, and is completely unscriptural as I have shown in this book, BUT IN BRIDER HERESY THAT COULD HAPPEN. Briderism gives an unscriptural elevated power to a sinner who is a pastor. This is in the realm of Nicolaitanism, which is the clergy over the laity. The Pastor has conquered the common person, and God hates it! Here is another example of this unscripturally elevated power. *The House of God*, by Hawkins and Ramsey; on page 46, states:

> "It [the Baptist Church] has been given 'keys' which represent a certain official authority of custodianship concerning the affairs of the

kingdom of heaven. This custodianship involves a 'binding' and 'loosing' activity. A part of this, we have seen, involves the purging of itself of insubordinate and sinful members, and this is to be and must be done by each specific localized church."

So according to them, you can now be purged out of the kingdom of Heaven. That's some power to wield over the heads of the laity.

Not only do Hawkins and Ramsey claim this power for the church, they go even farther and put the whole clergy in fear.

> "Whenever a church fails to execute its affairs in accordance with the will of Christ its head, its churchhood is in jeopardy - its 'candlestick' will be taken away unless it repents (e.g., see Rev.2:4,5). ...When a church becomes so corrupt that its majority decisions are contrary to the will of its head, Christ will no longer own it as His church. It loses its candlestick, its keys, its churchhood. No human being knows how many of the...house assemblies which have had their custodianships revoked."
> William C. Hawkins and Willard A. Ramsey, *The House of God*, (Simpsonville, South Carolina: Hallmark Baptist Church, 1980) 46-47

The result is a congregation motivated out of guilt and fear, instead of out of love and a free will. Another result is a clergy ruled by fear of going contrary to Jesus Christ, and thus causing his church to no longer be in the bride or the kingdom of Heaven. Out of a fear of compromise the pastor pushes harder, and becomes stricter than is necessary. Most of these new Nicolaitan commands end up having to do with the form of godliness on the outside, while missing the heart on the inside. The end result is a pastor and people living in fear constantly. 2 Timothy 1:7 says: *"For God hath not given us the spirit of fear; but of power, and of love, and of a sound mind."*

CHAPTER 8

SO, WHY BE BAPTIST?

To find the true line of believers, don't follow a denomination, follow the true word of God. In this book I have attacked a doctrine that is becoming more and more prevalent among the Independent Baptist Churches.

Let me say once again, I am a Baptist, and I am going to stay a Baptist because, aside from the Brider Heresy, the Baptist position is the scriptural position, and not all of the Baptist churches are Baptist Briders. I would say that the majority of them are not full Briders, who believe that only the Baptists will be in New Jerusalem and in the bride of Jesus Christ. I have seen many start to straddle the fence, and preach like a Brider, then say that after the rapture all saved will be in the bride and married to Jesus Christ. That's Dr. Hyles position in his book, The Church. I am a Baptist because of the distinct beliefs that have set the Baptists apart from all other churches down through the ages of the church. With this being said, I must say that I am a BIBLE BELIEVER, BEFORE I AM A BAPTIST.

My convictions come from the Book, not my denomination or church. The Baptist position is the scriptural position.

Why be Baptist?

The Baptists believe in separation of church and state. There may be some other churches that believe this also, but it has originated with the Baptists. Lutheran, Presbyterian, Anglican, and Roman Catholic all believe in a state church religion. Baptists do not. In Acts 18:12-17, we have an example of this with the deputy Gallio:

> "12 And when Gallio was the deputy of Achaia, the Jews made insurrection with one accord against Paul, and brought him to the judgment seat, 13 Saying, This fellow persuadeth men to worship God contrary to the law. 14 And when Paul was now about to open his mouth, Gallio said unto the Jews, If it were a matter of wrong or wicked lewdness, O ye Jews, reason would that I should bear with you:15 But if it be a question of words and names, and of your law, look ye to it; for I will be no judge of such matters. 16 And he drave them from the judgment seat. 17 Then all the Greeks took Sosthenes, the chief ruler of the synagogue, and beat him before the judgement seat. And Gallio cared for none of those things."

Oh, that we had a government that would do verse fifteen today! *"...look ye to it, I will be a judge in no such matters."*

Little by little, the United States Government is getting its hand into the business of the church, and it is a bad thing. It won't be long and Washington is going to tell us that we have to allow queers to teach in Sunday school, or that we can't preach on queers from the pulpit because it's hate speech. The farther we as a nation get away from the word of God and proceed into lawlessness, the more Washington is going to stick its nose in our business, and the more Rome is going to get its hand in our government.

A true Baptist believes that the government should stay out of the church's affairs, and the church should stay out of the government's affairs, except for the liberty to preach against the affairs of the state where they go contrary to the word of God. No church in this age has the biblical right to run the government, for that is the same thing that happens in South America, Rome, or Arabia. The church and the state are to be separate.

Why be Baptist?

Because the Baptists believe in the Autonomy of the local Church. By that I mean the local church runs itself, there is to be no outside power dictating what that local body of believers is to do. No head office meddling in the affairs of the local church, such as the Vatican in Rome, or the Temple in Salt Lake City. In 1 Corinthians 5 & 6 there are two different examples of decisions that are to be made by the local body of believers. One, of kicking somebody out due to immorality, and the other of someone defrauding the other, and settling it in the church, not before the unbelievers in a court of law.

Yes, Paul is writing to them and you might try to say that he is an outside influence. Yet he is the one who started this church and is instructing them on to a more established mature ministry. When mature, they will be run by no outside power, and even here they have the final decision to obey Paul or not to. This is common of a missionary church still getting advice from its founding missionary who instructs it until it becomes a fully indigenous work, independent of outside help or instruction.

Why be Baptist?

Because the Baptists believe in the Priesthood of the believer.

You as a born again believer have direct access to God, and go through no one else. This is a distinctive that is very important.

During the dark ages (they're called the "middle ages" now, but that is to make it not look so bad on the Roman Catholic church who ruled during this time), Rome told its followers that they had to go through their priest in order to get to God. But that is a doctrine from Hell to keep the people under the thumb of the Nicolaitans that were in charge at the time.

For you and I who are saved, we go through no one, but have direct access to God through Jesus Christ himself, who is God. *"For there is one God, and one mediator between God and men, the man Christ Jesus,"* (1Timothy 2:5).

You have direct access to God, and in that sense you are a priest. The blood that was shed on the cross opened up that way, and anyone telling you that you

So Why Be a Baptist?

must go through any other way is a Nicolaitan trying to get you back under bondage, and remove your liberty in Jesus Christ.

I also want to make the point here, that nobody can tell you what God's will is for your life. Others may see a certain call in you and can tell you what they think or what appears to be God's will for your life. Yet, the bottom line is that ONLY YOU can know what God wants you to do.

A pastor may mean well, but if God shows you something different than what your Pastor tells you then you are to go as God leads you. That doesn't mean to not listen to your pastor, for his advice is from years of experience and dealing with situations similar to yours. Often he will have scripture to give you to think about. BUT HE IS NOT GOD! Many a preacher has told a young man called to preach which school he ought to go to, usually the one the pastor went to. But if God leads you somewhere else you had better obey God.

Lately there has been a big push for parents to arrange marriages or even pastors to arrange marriages. A parent who checks out closely the one their daughter or son is dating is one thing. However, arranging the marriage, and not giving the child a final say is a dangerous thing.

Listen, nobody knows God's will for your life, and that includes whom you are to marry! The temptation we as humans get into, is when we are not quite sure what we should do, then we go and ask for advice. For me, that is when I got into the biggest messes. The Bible does say in the multitude of counselors there is safety. You ought to get advice, but only you can determine what God wants you to do. When you stand before the Lord at the Judgement seat of Christ you will give account to the

Here Comes The Bride
Lord, NOT THE BRETHREN!

In Acts 21 Paul should have listened to the brethren; but that was after the Holy Spirit had already told him not to go to Jerusalem (Acts 20:23). God can use a pastor, or the brethren, and will use the word of God and the Holy Spirit, but only you can determine what His will is for you.

I believe it is common, when you find what God wants you to do, for the brethren to usually disagree with you. You will look backslidden and out of the will of God.

How many good pastors are there in the ministry today, who, though they did right, their wife divorced them and God gave them another help meet and they remarried! Many of the brethren say these pastors are out of the will of God; yet in their hearts they know they are in the will of God, and God is using them. That's what bugs the once married brethren; God is using many of these divorced and remarried Pastors.

Why be Baptist?

Because Baptists believe in the eternal security of the believer.

That is, once you are saved you will always be saved. You cannot lose your salvation. Do you realize how many other denominations do not believe in this doctrine? All but the Calvinists, of course; they believe you are eternally secure even before you get saved, if you are one of the elect, which is heresy in the other direction from the Armenians.

If you are unsure about this doctrine then you need to go back and read what I wrote about you being in the body of Jesus Christ. If you are part of his body then you are in Christ, and HE CANNOT DENY HIMSELF (2

Timothy 2:13).

Why be Baptist?

Because Baptists will only baptize believers by immersion.

No infant sprinkling to eradicate the original sin, and all that baloney. I've written enough on baptism that nothing more here needs to be said. These five distinctives set the Baptists apart from all of the other religions in the world. These are the Biblical reasons for being a Baptist. Now, from that position there are many branches that shoot off in all directions, from charismatic Baptists, to Baptist Briders. These five distinctive doctrines will be common in all of the true Baptist churches, and some of the non-denominational churches that don't put the title of Baptist on their signs.

The Baptist position is the right position, but lately there has been a push of this Brider heresy in the Independent Fundamental Baptist churches. In the words of Benjamin Gilley:

> "By all means, LET'S BE BAPTIST. But for the Lord's sake, LET'S NOT BE BAPTIST-BRIDER!"
> Benjamin Gilley, *"Let us not be Baptist Brider,"* (Pensacola, Florida: Bible Believers Bulletin)

Here Comes The Bride

List of Sources
Alphabetically by last name

1. Dr. Ken Blue, *Baptist Briders Boloney* (Port Orchard, Washington, Local Church Publishing, 1997)

2. J.M. Carroll, *"The Trail of Blood,"* (Kentucky, Ashland Avenue Baptist Church, 1988)

3. Dr. Thomas Cassidy, *"The Bride, the Baptists, and the Bride of Christ"* (California: Spring Valley,1995)

4. Wayne Cox, *The Church* (Liberal, Kansas: Wilderness Voice Publications)

5. Herb Evans, *"The Body of Christ is Together,"* (The Flaming Torch, Vol.36, Number 6, October/ November/December 1995)

6. John Foxe, *Foxe's Book of Martyrs*, (Michigan: Zondervan Publishing House)

7. Benjamin Gilley, *"Let us not be Baptist Brider,"* (Pensacola, Florida: Bible Believers Bulletin)

8. Dr. Samuel C. Gipp, Th.D, *A Practical & Theological Study of The Book of Acts,* (Shelbyville, Tennesee: Bible and Literature Missionary Foundation)

9. Frank A. Godsoe, D.D.;Th.D., *The House of God A Blood-Bought Body*, (Del City, Oklahoma, 1973)

10. *"Golden State Baptist College Handbook,"* (Santa Clara California, 1997-98)

11. William C. Hawkins and Willard A. Ramsey, *The House of God,* (Simpsonville, South Carolina: Hallmark

Baptist Church, 1980)

12. Dr. Jack Hyles, *The Church*, (Hammond, Indiana: Hyles - Anderson Publishers)

13. Buell H. Kazee, *The Church and the Ordinances,* (Little Rock, Arkansas: The Challenge Press, 1972)

14. Rev. Clarence Larkin, *Dispensational Truth*, (Glenside, Pennsylvania)

15. James R. Love, *"The Bride,"* (The Flaming Torch, October, November, December, 1995, Rio Rancho, New Mexico)

16. Roy Mason, *The Myth of the Universal Invisible Church E-x-p-l-o-d-e-d,* (Little Rock, Arkansas: Challenge Press, 1978)

17. *Dispensational Truth*, North Star Bible Institute, no publisher but the Institute was at 1st Bible Baptist Church, Rochester, New York

18. Les Potter, *The Mystical Invisible Universal "Church"*, (Calvary Publishing, Lansing MI)

19. Alberto Rivera, *"Alberto"* (Chino, California, Chick Publications)

20. C. I. Scofield, *Scofield Study Bible* (Oxford University Press)

21. James Strong, LL.D.,S.T.D. *Strong's Exhaustive Concordance of The Bible* (Tennesee: Thomas Nelson Publishers, 1990)

22. Dr. Ron Tottingham, *"Baptist Brideism Is What?,"* (The Flaming Torch, October, November, December, 1995)

23. *Websters New World College Dictionary*, Third Edition, Published by Macmillan, USA.

www.ingramcontent.com/pod-product-compliance
Lightning Source LLC
Chambersburg PA
CBHW050123020526
44112CB00035B/2362